Evolutionary Magic

Magic

UNLEASH YOUR INNER POWER
WITHOUT SCARING THE NEIGHBORS

C.L. BIGGS

Publishing Services provided by Paper Raven Books LLC

Printed in the United States of America

First Printing, 2024

ISBN 979-8-9913518-3-6

CONTENTS

INTRODUCTION

Power.

This word can mean so many different things to different people. But what does it mean to you?

Money? Influence? Infamy? This is not a typical witchcraft or magic book about sacred dates, astrology, or candlework. You can just dip your toe in for the first time or be an advanced practitioner—either way, I've got something here for you. Anything and everything that you bring to the table to get you where you need to go is perfect, assuming it harms no one, including yourself. Darkness is not bad by any means, for it's the only way to see the stars. But everything I do, say, or write is for the purpose of peace on Earth and everywhere for all living beings and can only be used that way. 'Cus we're good like that. The more we know, the more responsibility we have, and the natural weight of that will not allow itself to be taken lightly. We all lose our temper or show our asses from time to time. I know I still do. The more we practice, the less we lose control. Practice means power.

Power means control. Maybe it's just the ability to control yourself from eating that donut. It refers to your ability to achieve something, without outside influence, using your innate Sorcery. You may have a lot of power, which you yield in your everyday life. Or maybe you grabbed ahold of this because you feel so desperately weighed down by the powerless situations you seem to find yourself in. Either way, I'm here for it. I'm here for you.

You have the power to take away someone's pain with a hug or a few loving words. You have the power to lend a hand to a person in need and get them through a crisis. You also have the power to make someone cry or break their heart, by telling them an ugly 'truth' no one really needs to hear. Power used is sacred and reaps results. Used for the lower frequencies that do not serve us, it just loops around until it can find a higher path. It can certainly do some damage while it waits for us to get on board, though.

As you go through these pages, you will discover or remember that there is another type of power inside of you, capable of achieving everything you've ever wanted. If you aren't getting what you want, ponder your real motives and sit with Dr. David Hawking's Map of Consciousness Frequency Scale (in the back of the book & on the website at www.evolutionarymagic.com). As you shift your frequencies, the effectiveness of a ritual or spell increases. The way to adjust yourself to the desired frequency can be as simple as taking a nap or dancing to your favorite song. Or it could be overcoming decades of conditioning. Magic is most potent in the allowing that occurs in the higher feeling states. Yet nuanced awareness to get there through muscle memory takes some work and commitment. We must be willing to let go of our expectations and funny enough, our attachment, to the goal. Point the ship to the coordinates and then busy yourself with the joy of adjusting the sails and seeing the beautiful ocean around you.

Through CONSCIOUS power, you can change the course of your entire life in terms of your health, happiness, and financial stability. The awareness of your Source Power can even radically change the whole world for the better should you choose to use it this way. Even if you don't, your happier life will have a greater effect on the whole. That's why I am here. I want you to have what you want so you can give me what I want: your blessings for a better world for all living beings. The better I can make your life, the more you will have space for the incredibly generous hearts that you are to focus your magical energy on the higher spells that are already in progress right now to heal and to renew our world.

A lot of people raise their eyebrows when we talk about magic and positive outcomes by design. How could they not? After all, everyone suffers in some way, shape, or form. Depression, anxiety, loneliness, poverty, hunger, illness—nobody is free of pain. So how can some miraculous bag of tricks truly exist? Read on, my friend. We are but a candle before the sun.

At its core, Source Power cannot be described, defined, or captured. So, we do our best. It's been called many things. Atman. That infinite power, connected to the Collective Energy that makes up reality, and so the world as we know it. What is water to a fish?

We are harmonizing this power inside of you, right now. It's your Magical Self, which has been waiting for you all your life anyway. You may have heard that higher voice from time to time, like a gut feeling or a whisper out of nowhere. You may already tap into it often, or this will be your first real adventure. Maybe you already rock your witchy vibes in bold, living color. Others of us are more subtle in our expressions. From deeply held beliefs or scarred-over wounds, we all have our reasons to live boldly or practice in the quiet. It is all absolutely perfect. Just be where you are.

I am probably going to piss off a lot of old-school Wiccans here, and while I don't mean to upset anyone, this is not a book on how to gather your herbs by the moonlight. There are plenty of really well-written books out there that do not need repeating. Here, you will discover some meditations, spells, rituals, potions, and tools you can use on this journey, but the mental and energetic work you're doing is the only real reason that you will come out a better Sorcerer. You can stand on your head and whistle Dixie and get the same results from anything I give you here, if that is your intention and power-filled focus. But this is a place to start so you can get in the habit of *consciously* wielding yourself. This is the ultimate nondenominational Sorcery book, and you will not find letter-to-the-law judgments here.

Our combined journey starts today—but fair warning... The door to your Magical Self doesn't stay open once it's unlocked. This book is a key, but the act of keeping the door open is up to you. Your commitment and self-grace will ensure the results you want. So practice your magic, learn more, really *use* your powers, and write in your journals, not just to improve your own life... to make the entire world a little (lot) better.

I

DISCOVERING

THE MAGIC MIRROR

"There are two ways of spreading light:
To be the candle or the mirror
that reflects it."

EDITH WARTON

Let's be real for a moment. Magic—what's the deal? There's a sense of mystery and, if we're honest, longing. Combined with a healthy bit of skepticism, most people hear "magic" and think of stage tricks or Hollywood sparkles. But I'm not here to pull a rabbit out of a hat (though, if that's your thing, go for it). This magic comes from deep inside you and is hidden so well that it is frightening. Spoiler: you're way more powerful than you think, and you don't need a ritual or wand to prove it.

There's a simple truth: life is messy. I'm guessing you've had your share of existential crises, cosmic plot twists, and mornings where even the coffee didn't seem to work its usual magic. We all have. So, why do some of us seem to rise above the chaos, weaving through life with ease, while others struggle? It's not some unattainable secret. It's magic. Or more accurately, it's about learning how to tap into the Source(ry) of You—the magic that flows through you. It's subtle, but once you see it, you can't unsee it. If you picked up this book, you already vibe in it. You know you have power and you want to make it better. More refined.

If you're expecting a typical how-to-witchcraft book with a side of astrology and moon charts, you may want to brace yourself. This is a different kind of journey. Magic is about power, but not in the wholly Wiccan way. It's not about wielding something external to control others. It's about harnessing control of our own thoughts, our emotions, our intentions—and learning to wield it in ways that will transform your life.

Sure, we'll get to spells and rituals. You'll find those here because they are fun. I like them to help us focus, and in many ways, it's how I got my start. But don't be fooled into thinking magic is about the right ingredients or the perfect sigil. Magic is about focus and intention. Sorcery is about feeling and emoting. All the tools of the trade are only helping you along. You can achieve the same results with a smile, a sigh, and a confident nod if you are truly tuned into your power. You can wear a robe and chant or be in your sweats with a cup of tea—it's all valid. We're after results, not theatrics. That being said... some ways are higher than others. This book is just an introduction.

This journey is about taking responsibility for your power. That's right—you're about to level up in self-accountability. With great power comes great responsibility; once you start this path, the door doesn't just close behind you. Your magic becomes the key, and how wide you throw it open is entirely up to you. Practice, focus, and intention will lead you to have control over your life in ways you maybe haven't contemplated before.

We'll start simple, with a mirror. But as with anything magical, simple doesn't mean shallow. You'll be meeting someone very important—your truest self. This is the part of you that already knows what you're capable of, even if the rest of you haven't quite caught up. Before some of you start to get your feathers fluffed that you already know yourself just fine, let me ask a question. Are you satisfied with the current unfolding of every area of your life? Seriously, happy... We all have some work to do. Well, there *are* humans who are pretty darn pleased with their lives, even if there are issues (there are always issues). But if you happen not to be one of those rare, lucky few, it's time to stop playing small.

So, here's to rediscovering your inner power, to unlocking doors you didn't even know existed, and to realizing that you're not just walking through life—you're creating it, spell by spell, thought by thought, breath by breath. You don't need to know all the answers right now. Just stay curious and keep moving. The magic is already inside you, and it's waiting.

Fortunately, you don't need a cauldron or a broomstick for what you're about to do. Caldrons can be tricky to clean and the best magic brooms tend to leave more twigs than a broom should. All you need is a mirror, a bit of courage, and a willingness to step into your true power. Because when you look into that mirror, you're not just seeing your reflection— you're seeing potential, possibilities, and a whole lot of untapped magic. Maybe you are seeing a serious entity in there, or maybe you don't see anything at all, and it seems to be sleeping. Be open and relax. Everything is going to be fine.

I want to go on record that I didn't make this ritual up. I was initiated into it. I share it with you as my offering that you become all that you can be in every aspect of your journey. I've taken my journey from deep oceans and valleys to miracles on a mountaintop. I leave at your feet the highest wisdom I have been so blessed to absorb in the hopes that you enjoy every bit and more of the expansion of the Universe and the power you have to expand it. I will leave notes in the back of this book if you want to look at the sources of my path later, but this is about your journey, and I'm excited to get to it. With this and every other practice in this book, I recommend reading through everything at least once before you do it in full range.

We could ease into magic slowly, but everyone wants results. So, yeah, we are going to dive right in. Tap into your Highest Self and wake up your innate magical attunements. Stir your innate Source up and get it moving through your awareness. We're beginning with the end. If you're an Atheist, no problem. Believe in the Goddess, God, or believe only in yourself? It is all perfect and empowering. Whatever you believe in, call yourself into it right now and become present with your divinity because for your very first ritual, we will be opening the door to a part of you that, right now, may remain hidden or sleeping—the part that is made of your innate Higher Power. Obviously, God doesn't need to be called to you, He/She/It clearly knows who and what you are. So, call yourself here and now into It— that which made all Life. Now you might feel a little spacey so ground yourself deep into the Earth by imagining a chord from about your belly button to the center of the Earth. It moves as you move and you are always completely, profoundly connected.

AWAKENING RITUAL: I AM THE LIGHT

"I Am a Divine Action of God, of Goddess. Here and now. And I Am Good."[1]

To get started, here's what you'll need:

- A mirror.
- Enough light to gaze into your own eyes.
- A little bit of privacy. Even ten minutes is great. 20-25 is ideal.

1. Stand or sit in front of a mirror and look deeply into your own eyes. Gaze at them. One, then the other. Slightly in the middle (third eye) that you can see both clearly. Relax your body and just gaze into your eyes.

If you have the privilege of privacy and can lay out some candles and gaze in a looking glass, excellent! If you have only ten minutes before you have to get the little ones to school, that is perfect too. Be content with what you have and strive to set aside more time to practice as you can.

2. Gently focus on your breathing, and as you breathe in and out, start to slow your breathing. Lengthen your breathing for three counts in and then four counts out, four counts in, and then five or six counts out. Soften your jaw, relax your tongue, and release your shoulders down as you continue to gaze into your eyes and breathe slow and easy.

3. Continue to focus your attention entirely on your own image.

As thoughts float in, allow them to float right on out. Don't worry; I'm sure they won't go far. You can think about the work you have to do or the dinner you need to make later. For now, focus on the point just between and above your eyes so you can gently apply pressure to the pineal gland. Soften your gaze a bit more and fall into the eternity that lies behind those magnificent eyes of yours.

4. Stay present and grounded by your own image. Breathe with yourself for a long time like this.

5. Soften your eyes a bit more and become very aware of your heart. You can place a hand over your heart even. See if you can feel your heartbeat through your body. Keep gazing into your eyes and relax the tongue once more. Feel the big feels here; feel love for yourself. Feel gratitude for yourself. Feel gratitude for your life, whatever it looks like here and now. If you can't find those feelings, feel love for your puppy or your kitten or whatever you adore and flood your body with that emotion and gratitude.

6. When you feel ready and are in a happy, elevated state, recite the following aloud to yourself (if you can without scaring people in the next room). Recite it a million times ideally— three times minimum.

"I Am a Divine Action of God(dess). Here and now. And I am Good. I am Kind. I am Enough. I am healthy and vibrant and open to the magic of the highest Love in my life. I am free."

7. When you are ready to complete this space, whisper thanks to yourself. Maybe give yourself a little bow in the mirror. You certainly deserve the honor. Whisper thanksgiving to the Divinity that you presenced before you began. Give another bow to This Beingness you called upon. Then start to come back into your body.

Move your hands up your opposite arms and feel yourself under your touch. Note your grounding chord and give it a warm thank you. Start to think about the things that make you the happiest. Ignore the world, if you can, for another 20 minutes while you integrate this incredibly powerful and phenomenally deep exercise. Dance. Laugh. Write about dreams that make you happy in your journal. Whatever brings you peace – enjoy it for a spell.

Need a quick pick-me-up after a particularly human day? Use an abbreviated version of The Magic Mirror above as a quick daily practice and certainly anytime you need to reconnect with this Higher Power that you are real quick.

When you aren't near a mirror and want to engage your Higher Self, flutter your eyes closed and gaze gently at your third eye while you run through the practice. And if all you can give it in any particular moment is just *One* breath, it is perfect. Go for it. Every conscious breath counts.

MAGIC BREATHWORK

Bring the breath deep into your body, grounding it in the stomach and pushing the solar plexus. Relax your shoulders. Once you get the hang of this, your shoulders shouldn't rise with your breathing. The breath lives in the belly.

Relax your jaw and tongue. Soften everything, and maybe your body will bless you with a released sigh or a yawn. Not only does the sigh feel incredible, but it signals that your body has attuned the nervous system to the intent. You're slipping into a more relaxed state that opens to higher awareness, and your body and brain are starting to harmonize with the breath and the spirit.

As you release the breath out, gently allow each breath out to be twice as long as the breath in and start to—pause—between each.

Eventually, focus your breath to breathe four beats in. Four beats hold. Four beats out. Four beats hold. Then, as you go deeper into your altered brainwaves, allow the exhalations to last as long as you can comfortably. An example of what that could look like…

Four counts in. Three counts hold. Six counts out. Three counts hold.

Four counts in. Four counts hold. Seven counts out. Four counts hold.

Six counts in. Five counts hold. Eight counts out. Five counts hold.

Play with it a little bit. You are not trying to 'hit a goal' here. You are learning to use the breath and letting the breath move and work inside you consciously.

Go on and try it. I'll hold. ☺

Now soften your eyes, relax your shoulders some more, and become aware of how you're feeling at this moment. Notice any tension in your physical body, and let's soften and release it deeper. Ground yourself deeply to the Earth and ground yourself more in the present moment by pulling everything you feel to the center of the body.

Take the tension and everything that doesn't serve you and gather it all up to move it up the center; up, up, up, and out the top of your head, releasing it to fall behind you, like a flowy bridal veil back to the Earth. Release it to the beautiful ground full of rich, lush grass. Now feel the Light and Goodness of Source Energy as the brightest White Light and release it from the center of your heart out to every cell in your body. Drench yourself in white light.

"I Am a Divine Action of God, of Goddess. Here and now. And I am so Good. My life is simple and easy, and I Am So Happy."

GURU DEV SRI ISA MAFU

Don't worry if it feels a little like a lie. You might be going through horrific trauma right now and aren't feeling it. The purpose of this ritual is to communicate well beyond the subconscious programming running the show.

> Did you know that your solar plexus, (located behind the aorta in the abdomen), mediates your stress response? It manages organs like your pancreas, liver, and gallbladder. These organs play a vital role in your emotions, believe it or not. Learning to activate this area when breathing is pure physiological magic at its best!

Give it the direction that you want to go.

You're telling your brain that even if you don't feel it, you acknowledge who you are and what you expect. It might take some time to make this feel true, which is perfectly okay. When you feel, you become. For now, you're welcoming a new sheriff to town.

Here is your badge, my friend:

As you bring this and any ritual to a close, always focus your attention on things that make you happy and give gratitude. Gently steer your thoughts to your goals and desires. Give the drama of today's news or the need to pay the bills at least 20 minutes on pause. Your subconscious is still listening. Feed it healthy thoughts to integrate this priceless ritual and direct the Universe to what it is you wish for.

CONJURE YOUR LIFE WITH INTENTION

"Magic is believing in yourself. If you can do that, you can make anything happen."

JOHANN WOLFGANG VON GOETHE

Let's talk about spells—not the "eye of newt, and toe of frog" kind, but the kind you cast every single day without even realizing it. You see, words are powerful. They carry weight, energy, and the ability to shape your reality. The term "spell" is often used casually, but if you dig a little deeper, you'll find that it's all about creation. When you spell something out, whether it's a word or an intention, you're putting energy into the world, crafting a reality that aligns with your thoughts and desires.

Spell. [_spel_]. From the Oxford Dictionary

verb

gerund or present participle: **spelling**

1. write or name the letters that form (a word) in correct sequence.

"Dolly spelled her name"

(of letters) make up or form (a word).

"the letters spell the word 'how'"

2. be a sign or characteristic of.

"she had the chic, efficient look that spells Milan"

3. mean or have as a result.

"the plans would spell disaster for the economy"

noun

noun: **spell**; plural noun: **spell**

1. a form of words used as a magical charm or incantation.

2. a state of enchantment caused by a magic spell.

"the magician may **cast a spell on** himself"

3. an ability to control or influence people as though one had magical power over them.

"she is afraid that you are waking from her spell"

Spell yourself silly; Spell yourself sane. Everybody spells all the time, but the conscious Spells are the most fun. We use the term spell often, and it means "to create" in the language we are currently using. Journaling is a clever and easy way to Spell your life into how you want it by focusing on what you already have, what you are grateful for, and what you wish to see (that feels light, easy, and attainable). Think about it—every word you speak is like casting a pebble into a pond. The ripples spread out, influencing the water's surface, just as your words influence your life. When you consciously choose your words, you're not just communicating; you're creating. You're spelling your life into existence, one thought, one word, one intention at a time.

But here's where the science meets the magic: language shapes our perception of reality. The words you choose can literally change the way your brain processes information. It's all about neuroplasticity—the brain's ability to reorganize itself by forming new neural connections throughout life. By intentionally using words that resonate with positivity, abundance, and possibility, you can rewire your brain to see opportunities where others see obstacles and to find peace in the midst of chaos.

In this way, journaling becomes more than just writing—it's a form of spellwork. As you write, you're spelling out your desires, your goals, your gratitude. You're telling the Universe, "This is what I want to create." And the Universe, ever the attentive listener, begins to align circumstances, people, and opportunities to make it happen.

Now, let's add a bit of rhythm to this spellwork. When you rhyme, something magical happens—your words flow with a natural cadence that taps into the deeper frequencies of your subconscious. Rhyming isn't just a poetic flourish; it's a way to embed your intentions even more deeply into your mind and spirit, making your spells more potent, more powerful.

So, as you spell your life, do so with care. Choose your words wisely, with intention, knowing that each one is a brushstroke on the canvas of your reality. Spell for the best in yourself and others, and watch as the magic of your words unfolds in your life. Remember, the Universe is always listening, so make your spells count.

CONTROL : WHO REALLY HAS IT?

"Believe in your heart that you're meant to live a life full of passion, purpose, magic, & miracles."

ROY T. BENNETT

Start your learning experience by asking yourself one key question:

"Am I truly in control over my own destiny?"

Some people will have no problem saying "NO" proudly. Sure, maybe you can make some choices at various points, but no matter what you do, the overall narrative is out of your control.

And for many people, this can even bring a lot of comfort.

They may feel that everything they ultimately do is predetermined by a superior force who knows and sees all. A person's job would then be to make sure they follow this path righteously, stay on course, and reach that destination— whatever it may be.

In fact, trying to take a U-turn from this path is often seen as silly or even blasphemous by those who hold this belief. Why would you even bother to fight destiny? Why would you focus your energy on saying no to God, or whatever other name you have for this superior power?

And then again, some believe the opposite. Call them "rebels" who refuse to even consider the fact that their entire lives are predetermined and that their choices have no say in where they ultimately end up. They believe that their destiny is entirely in their control, even if there really is a Creator who designed the very fabric of life.

So, before you continue reading this book, ponder the question:

"Am I truly in control over my own destiny?"

There is no judgment here, so don't be afraid to let your honest answer out even if you don't know. It is just important to reveal it for yourself because it may mean you might have to unlearn a false belief or any belief that has limited your mental space and ability to control your own path.

> In the early 70s, Dr. Bruce Lipton's work with stem cells demonstrated that the environment, rather than the genetic code, determined the fate of the cells. This means that our environment and "biology of belief" has a profound impact on the choice the cell makes to be healthy or sick. Mind over matter is not just a metaphor but a scientific reality. Perception rewrites our genes!

Because guess what?

YOUR FATE IS NOT PREDETERMINED, EVEN IF IT SEEMS AS THOUGH IT IS

Your fate is not written in some book, kept under closed doors by a celestial force that knows everything and looks at us from a distance. To build belief in your ability to change your life with magic, one has to have at least a basic, foundational understanding of the science that makes it possible and a belief that you have some power. We have been brainwashed by fiction in television and books that magic is marked by sparkly and instant physical manifestations. Or maybe a special spider bite. And while magic is real and remarkable, it is not flashy nor instantaneous.

A fascinating scope of science called Epigenetics[2] tells us that your physical body's fate doesn't have to stay locked up in your genes passed down by your parents. You have the power to change your 'destiny,' even if your whole family went down a particular path. I highly recommend *The Biology of Belief* by Dr. Bruce Lipton to give your brain some much-needed space to work in the higher realms. I could wax poetically about his and other greats' Epigenetic work in great length. Go look him up so you don't have to endure my nerdy fangirling. He's all over YouTube as well.

The bottom line is that your manifest destiny is up to you. This puts you back in the driver's seat and speeding right outta victim town. Talk about taking back your power.

The collective consciousness and its manifestation of power have been studied in depth, and while no one study can tag and bag a complete understanding, some very cool experiments show how collective consciousness can dramatically save lives, reduce crime, and bring peace, even to those who are not involved in the experiments. The Maharishi Effect is coined from a group of practicing transcendental meditators OM-ing out in the Washington DC area in June and July of 1993. I may seem to make light of this, but I am in humbled awe and respect of what they accomplished with their sacred practices. The study showed, "a 27-member independent Project Review Board consisting of sociologists and criminologists from leading universities verified the findings that the maximum decrease of violent crime was 23.3% when the size of the group was largest (roughly 4,000 people) during the final week of the project. The statistical probability that this result could reflect chance variation in crime levels was less than 2 in 1 billion (p < .000000002)."[3]

A 2016 peer-reviewed follow-up study[4] found an even larger decrease of violent crime reductions to 28.4% with roughly 1,725 participants and estimated that they prevented approximately 4,136 murders in the 206 cities studied.[5] Just, wow. When we are tapped into our Source-ry, we can change our lives dramatically. When we work together, we can move mountains.

To understand why, we must look closely at human DNA.

Science and spirituality are like two sides to the same coin. When they can put aside their differences, we all understand a bit more about the world. And scientific belief is evolving too. The Geologist Charles Darwin is often quoted from his theory of natural selection and the survival of the fittest as a justification for atrocious acts against fellow humans or animals. He reasoned that competition would help weed out the weak from the strong. However, as evolution was more thoroughly observed, it turned out that *cooperation* was the key[6], and even Darwin fully acknowledged this when he said, "Cooperation poses great problems for the natural selection theory." He wasn't sold on 'might is right' despite being continually cited as the grandfather of this justification for bullying in much of the 'modern' world.

Ironically, another geologist named Gregg Braden is one of my favorite presenters on remarkable scientific findings. He has an incredibly brilliant way of explaining what he thinks is the magic encoded in our DNA, and his groundbreaking research may have revealed an intelligent message encoded in the cells of all existence.

Braden began a project for the defense industry during the late 80s, in the midst of the Cold War. It was a time when the entire world was literally divided in two, and Braden wanted to show that, no matter their background or political beliefs, some common element connected all humans. He didn't even know what that "element" was then. But it seemed that Braden intuitively believed that humans must all be connected in spite of any apparent differences. Lucky for us he also had an extensive computer science background and wanted to dig in and find proof that people are connected.

He used the new Human Genome Project[7] for his research thinking that if we can imagine the incredible findings discovered about our own DNA as a library, with each strand of encoded sequence as a book, then there had to be a foreword or a table of contents somewhere. A note from the Author... some type of introduction.

In his book *The God Code*, Gregg Braden takes us on a journey into the very core of our being—literally. He specifically examines the connections between ancient alphabets and the elements in DNA, using Hebrew, Arabic, and Sanskrit to decode the message. Braden claims that the letters corresponding to the four bases of DNA—adenine, guanine, cytosine, and thymine—can be matched with these ancient alphabets. By doing so, he decoded a message that suggests a divine connection in our genetic makeup. His work emphasizes the idea that the same message is found across different cultures and languages, reinforcing the concept of a universal Creator or divine source present within all life.

His work suggests that within the strands of your DNA lies a hidden message from the Creator that speaks directly to the divine nature of who you are. Braden, blending ancient wisdom with modern science at its absolute base level, decodes the genetic alphabet and reveals something profound: the name of God, YHVH, is encoded in our DNA[8].

This isn't just an abstract concept. Braden links the ancient Hebrew letters to the elements that form life—hydrogen, nitrogen, oxygen, and carbon—and finds that when we translate these elements into their corresponding Hebrew letters, they spell out "God Eternal Within the Body." This discovery offers a powerful reminder that the divine is not just out there in some distant realm but is intricately woven into every cell of our being.

Braden's work is more than quite possibly the biggest scientific breakthrough ever; it's a call to recognize the divine power within us all. It resonates deeply with the belief that we are not merely participants in the universe but active co-creators capable of harnessing this divine energy to shape our reality. When you understand that your very DNA carries the signature of the Creator, you begin to realize the immense power you hold within yourself—the power to heal, to create, and to transform not just your life but the world around you.

I've provided the link to his YouTube video titled "The Code of Life Openly Hidden between the Lines of the Ancient Text" in the endnotes[9] and highly recommend the watch. It's less than 20 minutes and could completely change your entire perception of everything, but I also recommend the book. I do not get anything back from you reading it, but anything I can offer to help your mind wade through the old conditioning of not being 'enough' as a human helps us all.

"God Eternal Within the Body."

This is in line with several major Judeo-Christian beliefs that "God is in everything" and that humans are created in God's image. But this connection might be much more powerful than many initially believed. I want to be very clear here that I am not promoting any version of organized religion or any definition of God. I am proposing that You, Yourself, are indeed Divine.

This is the message that seems to be hidden within each minuscule cell of the human body in your DNA. These words don't just inspire the possibility that, indeed, a Creator has made humans in Their image, but that, perhaps, the actual source of Its immense powers lies within each person.

WHAT DOES ALL THIS MEAN?

*"Those who don't believe in magic
will never find it."*

ROALD DAHL

Ponder the possibilities of this message woven into the very fabric of your being and what that means for your own personal practice of magic and personal empowerment.

Apart from being a groundbreaking discovery or an interesting story to tell at the dinner table, it effectively supports the idea that you have been in control of your own destiny all along.

I understand that the impulse to resist this can be really (really) strong. It's downright treacherous to think we could have caused our own bad luck or terrible things to happen to us or others because of our thoughts and beliefs. I am not saying that a person chooses to be brutally victimized or give themselves cancer. What I am saying is that our thoughts and actions create circumstances that create cause and effect. Karma. There is a magic tool to resolve even the most difficult of karmas, but first, we have to understand that we do, in fact, have the power of creation. It's heartbreaking and empowering to embrace this. It gives us control and a cold shower.

Ultimately, it gives us access to our true internal power, our Source Power. It's because of this that I am so fond of the term Sorcery. Source-ry doesn't have the same historic negativity attached to it as witchcraft does. It boggles my mind that even today, in some places, there are people who would quite literally burn a woman (or a man) alive because they might have an advanced understanding of herbal remedies or basic astrological ramifications.

In major religious practices and psychologies, people are used to seeking help "outside" themselves and doing what they are told. In the West, we have been deeply conditioned to look at the sky and call out to a Divine being somewhere out there. We pray and ask for guidance. Many go through complex religious practices for their entire lives to feel closer to this Divine power. But in fact, this Divinity has been hiding right beneath our noses the entire time.

Thankfully, several religions also point to this greater truth. For instance, Kriya Yoga practitioners look inward to connect with God Spirit and believe that only by becoming more in tune with their inner wisdom and purpose can they truly live a life full of love, kindness, and peace. By meditating and searching deep within themselves, they connect with Spirit.

So perhaps intuitively, many other cultures and spiritual practices have sensed, at various levels, the presence of the Creator Spirit within human life. Several Eastern practices say just this.

Accepting this to be true will be one of the most difficult things we have to do if we have believed that God died on a cross and the only way to divinity is through another, invisible being who lived thousands of years ago. But learning (and accepting) that Spirit is within you also shatters the false belief that you are powerless over your life and your destiny.

There is Divinity in you, thereby magic. This means the Divine spark is yours to use to change the course of your life and the lives of people around you. Once we can accept who we are, we can go about creating a world we want to live in. I've got spells and goodies in here for you to work with to help integrate the higher truths, but please understand that these are a bridge to your more advanced practice. The higher you go, the more miraculous changes you will observe. Sometimes, only in hindsight. It's funny that we walk through opportunities without so much as a backward glance of thanks when we prayed and wished so incredibly hard for them way back when. Our manifestation memories can be quite short.

Crystals are a hard mineral that our current science does not measure differentiating frequencies from. However, you would be hard-pressed to tell anyone sensitive to them that they aren't supporting different healing benefits. Some of my best friends are crystals! The point (pun intended) is that our science and widely held spiritual beliefs are still very much in their infancy in many ways compared to our seemingly 'advanced' culture. Holding the space in your mind that we know a fraction of what makes our world tick will allow your brain the neuroplasticity it needs to heal, grow, and expand in its awareness. After all, it was only in 1889 that the Commissioner of the US Patent Office wanted to shut it down, thinking that "everything that can be invented has been invented." That was, of course, before the typewriter, telegraph, and telephone were invented. Forget computers and the internet! This is why keeping a humble, open mind is so vital to growth.

CAN YOU REALLY HAVE THAT CONTROL?

"Only those who will risk going too far can possibly find out how far one can go."

T. S. ELIOT

Think of the things you used to love as a child, like painting or singing. Bring that memory forward, then ask yourself— when was the last time you did that same thing, with the same levels of passion and joy you used to have when you were younger?

If you remember a recent moment you did just that, you are really lucky. Most people probably cannot say the same. This life is noisy and often takes us away from harnessing any ability that is not deemed "useful" by society. We're also drenched in technology and distracted away from our own creativity by our social media feeds. Five more minutes of fluffy bunny shorts can magically turn into an hour. I get it.

Only the little girl who filled her room with her beautiful watercolors grew up into an incessantly busy lawyer who never sketches anything ever anymore. The boy who spent most of his time inventing chilling adventures in his backyard grows up to be a man who rarely leaves his desk and forgets to daydream about other worlds.

Well, the person reading these words right now has experienced exactly what those children did. You see, the question isn't "Can you control your destiny?" but "Will you do it?"

The powers of control are already inside of you. It's literally written in your DNA, the very fabric of your being, and nothing can change that. But just because we possess the ability to do something doesn't always mean we will actually use it. It doesn't mean you will put in the effort to cultivate it, learn its limitations and abilities, and what you can do with it. The thing is—it's okay to be okay with where you are.

It takes time and requires patience. With yourself and your practice.

It requires a promise you make to yourself that you are willing to put in that effort now and start tapping into your natural abilities. The results are so very worth it because once you tap into it, the possibilities are endless.

After all, you have a piece of the Creator Magic inside every single cell of you. It is Wisdom, Guidance, and Love, and it is always there. Maybe you don't know how to look inward and tap into them yet. Maybe you do and want to progress your already advanced skills.

Let us make this an amazing ride together. Let's change the world.

What this book can't do, nor can anyone else for that matter, is do the work for you. Growing yourself spiritually is an active process. You will need to make time for it in the little moments of awareness that creep up. You may need to spend some of your resources on it. Yeah, I mean—we are talking about effort. Your success next year is determined by this minute and the next. But you are not alone.

I know, I know. Self-discipline is a bitch. But it is oh so worth it. And since I am granting my own magic to yours, I must practice what I preach. Bugger. I guess we really all are in this together.

You need to make your future self the promise that you will follow through. Then, break the promise immediately so you can relax about it all. Dissolve the karma of broken commitment by getting it over with and then buckle down and find the joy in the journey. After all, of all the secrets of the study of the Mysteries, using your *feelings* as your beacon of success is one of the most prolific secrets to know. Guilt and shame have no place here.

CLOSING RITUAL : (NEW) MOON BATH

Now that you have been reminded who is really in control of your destiny, it's time to celebrate the new chapter you will soon be writing.

And the best way to do just that is during a New Moon with a ritualistic bath!

The New Moon is all about fresh starts and setting strong intentions for the next cycle, which is exactly what you need right now.

If it's not a New Moon today, don't worry—you can still perform the ritual and enjoy its benefits, then replicate it every New Moon to establish a stronger connection to your spiritual commitment. Or advance your practice and bend time. Seize a new moon in your awareness and move yourself in spirit to that time, and do the ritual inside this space in your mind. Space and time are on the same continuum, so not only is it possible with intent, but it is also a powerful sorcery to practice. Burt Goldman, author of more than 20 books, calls it Quantum Jumping and teaches some great techniques in the practice. Either way, the point is to make yourself "New". You can do this every single day if you wish.

Here's a great way to tap into a new you:

1. Run a hot bath. If you can't, fill a bowl with some warm water and use it to cleanse your face. The power is in the intention and way you can make yourself FEEL.

2. Grab a cup of salt, which has incredible cleansing properties. You can also add your favorite essential oils if you want. I will talk more about these later, but when you use them, add them with purpose and intent. Where your mind goes, your energy flows.[10]

3. Add your ingredients to your bath and focus on your spiritual commitment to reclaim control over your destiny. Say these words out loud:

"I Am a Divine Action of God. I am loved. I Am Love. I clear the way now for my highest path for health, awakening, and happy abundance for myself and all others who would wish the same.
I wash away all that does not serve me and
fill the space with love & light.

Thank you, thank you, thank you."

You don't *have* to say 'thank you' three times, but when I get started, I often become a puddle of gratitude. Gratitude is one of the higher frequencies at 541MHz, which resides on the Consciousness Frequency Scale in the field of Oneness and

Self-Realization. Remember, this is in the back of the book and an incredibly helpful tool. Use it. Own it.

Not only does gratitude work to manifest what you're spelling—it bathes your body in a healing frequency and uplifts those around you. These mantras and simple meditations will help awaken the Divine part of you that can achieve all your deepest desires. You can repeat this incantation as often as you continue the ritual or anytime you wish.

4. Get in the bath or gently wash your face with the salty water. If you are bathing, be sure to gently salt cleanse all the crevices of the body. The bends in the elbows, knees, etc. Imagine yourself salting away anything dark or that no longer serves you. It absorbs and absolves.

5. Meditate for a few minutes while in the water about what your future will look like as you achieve your goal. Integrate this focused vision and activate the senses. What does it feel like? Look like? Taste like? Smell like? Sound like? Own your imaginings. Roll around and play in them. Get lost in it. Breathe it into your cells and from your cells. Be grateful for the amazingness of its manifestation as if it had already happened.

If you're using the bowl, soften your eyes, gaze at the water's surface, and do the same.

6. Wash your face and your body to get rid of all the emotional or mental blockages that could keep you from achieving your spiritual pledge. Get that crud all off and out of you. If you find yourself in fear or anxiety, no biggie; take a step back and shake it off. You can't break anything here. You are safe and protected because your intention is to do no harm to yourself or anyone else. Literally, get out and shake your body and move chaotically till you release the angst and then warm the water and go in again.

7. When you feel complete in the practice, get out of the tub and watch the water slowly go down the drain as you towel off and get comfortable. Enjoy the flow of the water out of the tub. After all, it is removing all your blockages from your body and your path. It is taking your dreams and releasing them to the world beyond to be evaporated into magic bits of manifesting glory.

Imagine everything that you're letting go of just washing right down that drain. Scatter the warm and fuzzy juju you're feeling into every bit of your being and give yourself that 20 minutes or so to integrate the good feelings before you wander back into the world.

Repeat this ritual every New Moon, or whenever you feel you need to recommit to your spiritual commitment, or when you need to wash away anything that gets built up on you.

Endnotes

1. Foundation for Meditative Studies. "About Guru Dev Sri Isa Mafu." Accessed August 13, 2024. [http://www.foundationformeditativestudies.org/aboutus/about_mafu.shtm].

2. Lipton, Bruce, and Ron Ehrlich. "Epigenetics & Healing – Dr. Bruce Lipton with Dr. Ron Ehrlich." Dr. Ron Ehrlich, February 2, 2024. [https://drronehrlich.com/dr-bruce-lipton-a-new-hope-epigenetics-and-the-subconscious-mind-2/].

3. Maharishi International University. "Reduced Violent Crime in Washington DC." Accessed August 13, 2024. [https://research.miu.edu/maharishi-effect/reduced-violent-crime-in-washington-dc].

4. Princeton University. "The Peace Intention Experiment." Accessed August 13, 2024. [https://noosphere.princeton.edu/peace.intention.html].

5. EurekAlert! "NEWS RELEASE 30-MAR-2017 Follow-up Study Suggests Group Meditation Reduced Murder Rates in Large US Cities." Accessed August 13, 2024. [https://www.eurekalert.org/news-releases/511271].

6. Wikipedia. "Cooperation (Evolution)." Accessed August 13, 2024. [https://en.wikipedia.org/wiki/Cooperation_(evolution)].

7. National Human Genome Research Institute. "The Human Genome Project." Accessed August 13, 2024. [https://www.genome.gov/human-genome-project].

8. Braden, Gregg. *The God Code: The Secret of Our Past, the Promise of Our Future.* Carlsbad, CA: Hay House, 2004.

9. Braden, Gregg. "The Code of Life Openly Hidden Between the Lines of Ancient Texts." YouTube video, 1:20:15. Posted August 13, 2024. [https://youtu.be/jMtt8Wvm1NM].

10. The quote "where your attention goes your energy flows" has been attributed to both James Redfield (Author of the *Celestine Prophecy*) as well as Tony Robbins, although I suspect that notion has been around long before either of these brilliant men were born.

WHAT IS YOUR POWER?

"The world is full of magic things, patiently waiting for our senses to grow sharper."

W.B YEATS

Power. It's one of those words that gets thrown around a lot, often misunderstood, and sometimes misused. But what if I told you that real power isn't about dominance or control? It's not about bending others to your will or collecting accolades like shiny trophies. Real power is something far more subtle, more profound, and—dare I say it—more magical.

You see, power isn't about what you can take; it's about what you can give. It's about the energy you carry within you and how you choose to share it with the world. But here's the kicker—most people don't even realize they have it. They walk through life, feeling small, insignificant, and powerless, never knowing that they hold the key to something truly extraordinary.

So, let's flip the script. Instead of asking, "What can I get?" let's ask, "What can I create?" Because that's where your true power lies—in your ability to create, to transform, to bring something into existence that wasn't there before. And no, I'm not talking about conjuring a rabbit out of a hat (though if you can do that, I'm thoroughly impressed). I'm talking about creating change, both within yourself and in the world around you.

The great secret that the wisest witches, mystics, and sorcerers have known for centuries is this: Power begins from within. It starts with self-awareness, with understanding the energy you carry, the light that shines within you, and how to amplify it. It's about recognizing that you're not just a passenger in your own life—you're the driver, the navigator, the one who decides which road to take.

But before you can wield this power, you need to tune into it. Like a radio station that's just a little bit off the dial, your frequency needs to be adjusted. You need to clear away the static, the noise, the self-doubt that's been playing in the background for far too long. And that's where the magic happens—when you finally hear the clear, true sound of your own power, humming within you like a well-tuned instrument.

This isn't just about feeling good; it's about aligning with your true self, your highest potential. It's about tapping into the energy that's always been there, waiting for you to notice it. And once you do, well, that's when the real fun begins.

Before we dive into the ritual that will help you refuel your magical energy, take a moment to ponder this: What if the power you've been seeking has been within you all along? What if, instead of looking outside for validation, approval, or permission, you decided to claim what's already yours?

You don't need a magic wand or a spellbook (though those are always fun to have around and I highly recommend you keep a record of all of your spells). What you need is the courage to look within, to acknowledge your own strength, and to understand that your power is as natural as the air you breathe. It's there, waiting for you to notice it, to embrace it, and to use it in ways that will amaze even you.

So, as we prepare to step into the next ritual, remember this: Your power is not something you have to earn or prove. It's something you already possess. It's a gift, a birthright, and it's up to you to decide how you're going to use it. The only question that remains is— are you ready?

RITUAL : MAGICAL REFUEL

This short visualization exercise will help you see the power that lies within you. It will fuel every cell of your body and bring more awareness into how much you can accomplish once you set your mind to it. This particular practice seems deceptively simple but can be one of the toughest for those with an undisciplined mind. You might find it helpful if you record it into your phone and play it back as a self-guided meditation.

Here's what you need to do:

1. Go to a quiet place, either in your home or somewhere in nature. Set your intention. What are you looking to create for yourself?

2. It's best to do this ritual when you're all alone, so you can focus on it. Make it somewhere that you won't be disturbed or wait till everyone else in the house is asleep.

3. Lie perfectly still in a position you feel most comfortable in, such as flat on your back, or in your favorite chair. Use caution lying down. It's easy to fall asleep with an untrained mind, and this won't get you where you want to go. If you want me to be real with you, I would say that you would want to sit as close to full lotus as possible and elevate your tooshie just a bit to release your knees down, aligning the chakric centers into their highest geometric position. There is a reason the highest yogis sit like this. But sit where you can be comfortable and work your way to whatever your personal yogi posture looks like to you.

4. Close your eyes and bring your awareness to your breath. Make your spine as tall as possible and work your breath through the center.

5. Try to push out any distracting thoughts. For this moment, all you need to think about is how the air is entering and exiting your body. The highest magic ALWAYS lives within the breath.

6. When you feel ready, start to imagine a bright golden-white light coming from just above your heart.

7. The light is slowly growing until it covers your entire body. Beautiful, electric, white light.

8. See it with your mind's eye as it's covering your chest, neck, face, arms, legs, and every inch of your physical vessel. Breathe it in and breathe it out.

9. Then, imagine this light is expanding even more, and covering your environment. Lift yourself into the sheer pleasure and peace of the practice. Enjoy it and nurture the feeling of happiness in the light, as the light.

10. This light is your Power. It starts from within, but it can affect the world around you if you let it and as you work the techniques to expand it.

11. Stay with this golden-white light for a while and make a note of what you are feeling as it moves in and through your body. Remember your feelings are your barometer of the success of the ritual.

12. Focus on what your intention is and now breathe this happiness-charged white light into your intention. See it glow before your mind's eye. Feel the vision charge with your life force of White Light Sorcery. See it play out exactly as you wish it and then release it to the Universe.

13. Focus your awareness back into your body and breathe in and out that happiness, the joy of the reward without attachment to it. Let it go and bask in the feelings a bit.

14. When you're ready, gently stretch back into your body and slowly open your eyes. Please remember to allow yourself 20 minutes of your mind wandering only within happiness and peace, compassion and joy. Gently guide your subconscious into the happiness of your completed intent. Continually bring your awareness to peaceful things.

Give gratitude and spread the intention to all others who would want to achieve it. Be happy.

You are now ready to experience the next chapter. We're going to get through some housekeeping in there, so be patient. It isn't uncommon to experience doubt when performing your practice, and we need to address some of the things that bounce around in our heads and distract us from our intentions. It's better to get it out of the way while you're relaxed and reading now so that when you're in the middle of a practice, you have the ammunition you may need to hush the doubts that pop up like little demons of doubt at very inopportune times.

WHAT DOES IT MEAN TO HAVE MAGICAL POWERS?

"I am sure there is Magic in everything, only we have not sensed it enough to get a hold of it and make it do things for us."

FRANCES HODGSON BURNETT

Moving objects with your mind.

Hearing other people's thoughts.

Levitating from the ground.

Shifting into a different person or animal.

These are just some examples of "magical powers" that most people can think of. They are also a few of the many powers featured in the X-Men comic books, as well as a handful of other supernatural fiction. All superheroes have powers. It's almost hard not to be envious.

Did you know that the human brain can process 11 million bits of information every second, but our conscious minds can only handle 40-50 bits of information per second?

It's in there...

The idea of magical powers can seem quite silly if you envision only what has been featured in pop culture. Magic, in the way you see on the screen, does not exist. But real magic (often spelled with an extra k for distinction that I use interchangeably) is very much real. In fact, there are supernormal powers that great meditators have claimed (and demonstrated) to achieve. In "The Yoga Sutras of Patanjali," there are eight supernormal powers. Most of the powers portrayed in science fiction actually stem from one of these eight and have been documented at some point by great monks. They have spent lifetimes attuning to the higher frequencies and practicing very specific techniques to get there.

I once heard of a woman who was meditating so hard she transmigrated herself to her front porch. The whoopsie of it was her doors had been locked and her keys inside. Another amazing story that I have been told by several people who were present and took part in the chanting for a woman who broke her neck diving into a pool with a layer of ice on the top. They continued to chant for her, and not only did she survive, but her X-rays showed the break when she was brought into the hospital. They also showed no sign of it when she left. Using that same chant, I personally watched a woman bring a little unresponsive, seemingly dead frog back to life.

I have experienced a great many psychic phenomena and had several jaw-dropping miracles in my own life. But I have just barely tasted the limitless potential of the Supernormal Powers of the Sutras. Are they real? Yes. Just a lick of power has unequivocally convinced me of the truth of, well, the truth. But I have never magically landed myself on the front porch. (Though I did "fall" through a floor in my spirit-body once. That was a trip!)

The real practice of magic involves raising and directing energy to fulfill a person's intentions and desires. Both spiritual individuals and scientists can agree that everything contains energy—nature, animals, people, and even objects. $E=mc^2$ means that energy is everything. If we break down what energy is, being everything and all, it is defined as Source/God manifest in physical.

As a result, magic aims to leverage this world-building energy as a way to make something come to physical manifestation. And everyone has innate magical abilities that can help them achieve this if they choose to harness them.

Curiously enough, most people already take part in lots of magical activities even if they don't realize it. The average manifestation of magic is very subtle but incredibly powerful.

Have you ever meditated as a way to relax after a difficult day? Meditation is magic in its purest form—it uses your own energy to calm your mind and soul to achieve the relaxation needed to create whatever you wish to focus on. I've heard it said there is a different meditation for every day, even as you cannot step into the same river twice. There is no right or wrong way to meditate, but there are definitely techniques that get you where you want to go faster. And others that are just relaxation.

Or have you ever tried manifesting with the Law of Attraction? This is a very common form of abstract magic, where you're using your cell energy to claim something you want.

Ask and you shall receive. Feel and it is given. Very good stuff.

Focus your energy on your desire and you will bring it closer to your reality through the laws of attraction. The next book in this series will go deep into the several laws of manifesting that are part of the universal laws of attraction. That isn't a quick conversation, or everyone who focuses on a purple elephant would have one suddenly appear in their room. Still, it's a conversation very much worth having and is deeply tied to Sorcery at its core.

Magic makes up our world. It makes our dreams come true, protects us from the things that go bump in the night, and allows us to grow as individuals. But most people don't agree with this statement because they have not actually accepted their magical side. They didn't get that elephant to suddenly appear in their room so they think maybe none of it is real.

When you ignore magic and the abilities you have, you're essentially leaving everything to chance and telling your subconscious you have no power. So it's no wonder so many people are unhappy with their life circumstances. They're refereeing their own life from the sidelines and not actually playing the game. Then they are wallowing in the loss of their most innate abilities without understanding, all the while creating more of what they don't want.

If you decide right now, to get in the field, would that work? Well, technically, yes, it absolutely would, but the answer could be more complicated. We want to keep this as simple as possible, but there are "more things in heaven and earth than can be dreamt of in the imagination." Getting in there and staying there are two different things.

WHO CAN PRACTICE MAGIC?

"*Magic is really only the utilization of the entire spectrum of the senses. Humans have cut themselves off from their senses. Now they see only a tiny portion of the visible spectrum, hear only the loudest of sounds, their sense of smell is shockingly poor, and they can only distinguish the sweetest and sourest of tastes.*"

MICHAEL SCOTT

The energy that makes your body and its connection to the Creator gives you the birthright to see the results of your magical labor.

There is no limitation as to who can practice magic, no matter its form. Some types of magic may be easier to perform for the uninitiated, such as simple meditation or prayer. Others, like spellcasting, need a bit of practicing because one is then basically holding a delta/theta wave-soaked brain while physically moving and chanting. Transcending and participating in a physical activity is not for the uninitiated or lazy. Neither is advanced transcendent meditation. These days, I personally find my favorite rituals now involve being completely still and wholly absorbed in specific meditative techniques and integrations. I still absolutely love a good ritual, but it's the deeper meditations that do it for me the most. Holding transcendence while gazing at the flame... now we're talking!

What separates the most successful practitioners is self-awareness, confidence in their practices, and the belief in their powers. Confidence comes from scoring wins in practice. Experienced witches, warlocks, and sorcerers know that they possess the ability to harness their energy and set their intention to achieve a goal because they have experienced it working in the past. It's easier to win a game when you know for certain that a game can be won. Those wins build Momentum that is not only powerful in itself but also its own universal law of manifestation.

We use this awareness and turn it into different actions, such as casting spells, blessings, reciting prayers, or making a potion. These actions are further ways for a witch to harness their energy and form a strong intention. It's all about intention. And the breath. People of all genders, sexes, races, and religions can score a few wins and be highly successful. Magic does not discriminate, nor is it reserved for just anyone. The world of Spirit is the ultimate "leave no one behind" practice. The more you open your heart, the stronger you will become.

Okay, I saw you perk up there when I mentioned potions. A potion is (generally) a collection of herbs, oils, and other goodies with specific frequencies that are combined with purpose, intent, and focus. It's a liquid that can heal, attract, or harm. They can be simple or quite complex. One can use it for any number of things and feed off the energy or use it to power another ritual. Potions are one of my favorite things to make, and I created a small following making them for everything from weight loss and stress relief to releasing toxic, righteous anger.

I have a whole blended bunch to heal emotional turmoil. I have become discerning with the base ingredients I use for them, and along with the occasional fresh herbs, the highest frequencies I can get are with medicinal-grade essential oils. I'm also a big fan of the original Bach Flower Remedies, and I often blend them as tincture potions for friends and family. I feel incredibly privileged to live in a time and place where I can order potent, clean tinctures to my door. Sure beats traipsing through the fields in the middle of the night in the full moon to gather the herbs and then process them through days of effort. I mean, really—how lucky are we?

MONEY, MONEY... WHEREFORE ART THOU?

"Money is usually attracted, not pursued."

JIM ROHN

Naturally, the best materials are not cheap. But do not get caught up in thinking your spell won't work because you're using store-bought dried herbs. It does not matter. The evolution of magic is always increasing in quality and form. I certainly did not start off with the good stuff. I scrounged for whatever I could use at a very young age, and through many fits and starts, I evolved by recognizing the wins and holding dear even the smallest results. Begin where you are; you are Divine. The details will take care of themselves as you evolve in your practice. The cleaner you get about manifesting money, the more money you will have to play. But if you do not clear the blockages you have around money, you will have bigger bills that eat up your rewards. You will find several ways to attract money in this book because I want to see you very wealthy, healthy, and wise. The richer you are, the more generous you can be.

The psychology of clearing away what doesn't serve your mind is every bit as important as writing a spell. Well, no— it's much more so. We've got to get our heads on straight to get to where we want to go. Use potions and Bach Remedies to help clear emotional and mental blockages around money, health, and your spiritual awakening so that you can manifest cleaner, bigger, and better. Support your magical evolution with your practice like the most compassionate parent of the cutest puppy and make ways for yourself to heal what needs healing. Redirect your yappy little thoughts to release and forgiveness when they turn bitter. Dial into the very small nuances of your emotions and shine the Light. Don't let them cower in the dark to grow three heads. Heal what comes up as it does. The ripple effects will be huge. There are no shortcuts to getting around the need to heal your blockages, but there are ways to speed up the healing by being aware as you come across them. Awareness brings peace and peace creates the garden for your manifestation and magic to thrive and deliver your hopes and dreams.

My goal isn't to give you a black-and-white recipe of required things you need to make a potion, but the ability to make your own with what you happen to have around or can acquire. I have come to learn that focused intention, mental imagery, brainwave work, and breathing techniques are a far greater path to and indicator of success than which physical tools are actually used to focus your intention. I love potions because they can be very simple and supportive. For example, let's look at an easy money-drawing potion. You can use as many or as few ingredients as you can easily obtain. I'll give you some of the most potent, but your intention makes this next little number shine.

A GREAT MONEY-DRAWING POTION

We will talk more about money later too, but since we're on potions, let's go for it.

Here is what you need:

- Choose your favorites from the highest money-attuned essential oils you can easily find: Orange, Frankincense, Patchouli, Clove, Ginger, Myrrh, Cinnamon, and Black Spruce are among the highest.

- A roller bottle with Citrine chips that have been cleaned carefully with water and your visualization of White Light from your being. Take a moment to 'charge' them with all your good meditative money juju, intention, and visualization. Sit with this till it feels completely cooked.

1. Use your 'magic breath' breathing technique. After spending some time getting in the "money comes to me so effortlessly and easily mood" and vibing strongly in that frequency, mix whichever of the above oil beauties you collected together.

2. Fill a little roller bottle with your tiny Citrine chips.

3. Pour in your oil blend. You can use about 10-12 drops each or go by the smell you wish to create. Then, you can add a carrier oil to top it off. The best ones to use for this would be almond or grapeseed oil (or both), which are both associated with money, prosperity, and success.

4. As you work with it and then every time you use it, repeat with humble gratitude over and over again the phrase,

"Thank you! I love that money comes to me easily, constantly, unexpectedly, and abundantly. Money is my friend. I receive, save, and give with ease. Thank you!"

Fall in love with money and release the resistance as it crops up. Forgive where money has failed you and move on. Your past has nothing to do with your future. Let it go and make space for your new reality.

TRADITIONAL MONEY DRAWING

Another oldie but goodie ritual for money is blowing cinnamon across your door's threshold on the first of every month. It does make space for money to flow because you're taking the time to vibe that frequency through your door.

It also can be toxic to cats, so you need to be mindful of this. And for goodness' sake, please do not use any potions on your animals unless you thoroughly research each and every ingredient to ensure they are not toxic to the little fellows. Be mindful that their sense of smell is far more potent, and they may not enjoy smelling like patchouli all day. For best results, do not force your will on anything or anyone.

SORCERY IS FUN... AND A GREAT RESPONSIBILITY

"Black magic is not a myth. It is a totally unscientific and emotional form of magic, but it does get results-of an extremely temporary nature."

ALEISTER CROWLEY

Whenever someone brings up magic, the topic of "white vs. black magic" always comes up. Yes, both of them are real, but like magic itself, neither of them works like what you may have seen in the movies, and while you do need to be responsible, please toss the whole idea of not using it for your own personal gain out of the first window you can find.

Use it. Love it. It is Universal power and it is yours for the taking because you are made up of it.

Think of "magic" as a set of tools. How one uses these tools is an entirely personal decision—you can use the hammer in the toolbox to help build something great, or you can use it to smash something into a million pieces.

In American history, the division of "black" and "white" magic doesn't refer to spells that are good or bad. This division has quite a racist history, with the term "black magic" being commonly used in the West to describe African rituals and religions, such as hoodoo.[11]

Black magic, as a term, was used to describe the parts of African Religion that seemed most strange to outsiders. This effectively created the notion that "black magic" is "evil," an idea so deeply imprinted into the collective consciousness that we still see it in pop culture today.

Of course, one can certainly use magic to perform "evil" or "bad" acts, but it won't get you very far. This is where the role of personal responsibility comes in. Witchcraft has no morality, but the person casting the spells certainly does. We are not going to get into the subject of demonology because this isn't that book, and we have no part of that here. Remember, peace on Earth and everywhere for all living beings. We call darkness into the light. All darkness into the light. Anything that chooses to remain darkness cannot exist in the light, and so it's none of our business.

If you choose to tap into your Divine powers and use magic, it's important to consider the ultimate goal you're working towards:

Is it to make your own life better, and fulfill your dreams?

Or is it to make others' lives worse?

Like magic itself, these questions don't have black-and-white answers. Everyone has moments where they give into greed, selfishness, or other dark feelings buried deep inside of them. And they can also have pure, loving thoughts, and want to give something back to the world.

If you are drawn to so-called "black magic," or magic that is designed to cause harm to someone else, chances are you are in a really dark place. And unfortunately, the Universe has a way of countering any negativity you put out there with your magic. You won't like the results. One of the most powerful symbols of Sorcery is the Ouroboros. It's the dragon or serpent eating its own tail. The symbolism goes beyond the cycle of birth, life, and death. The primordial energy we put out is what we feed upon. The Egyptians called the Ouroboros "Sata," and it surrounded the world with protection against cosmic enemies. That's pretty forward-thinking for an ancient civilization. This sacred circle has no beginning nor end and is one of the most clean and direct symbols of the manifest life cycle I know of. We reap what we sow, and while it looks weird as a visual, when it comes to what you choose to put out into the world, consider it the food you will partake of next.

BALANCE & BEAUTY IN CONSCIOUSNESS

On the other side of the coin, we find the power of intention, a precious arm of magic that has been demonstrated scientifically by many. Some of the most thrilling experiments on the power of consciousness come from Lynne McTaggart's research work[12] on the interconnectedness of all things and the power of the mind over reality. She has done numerous peer-reviewed experiments that involved collaboration with scientists from prestigious universities. Her work, particularly the "Intention Experiments," has been scientifically controlled and has demonstrated human intention can affect physical reality. She has built an incredible reputation and demonstrated statistically significant changes including increased plant growth rates, altered molecular structure in water, improved health outcomes in participants, and even bringing peace to a war zone.

In 2008, McTaggart managed to organize about 15,000 participants from 60 different countries to focus on peace for ten minutes a day for a week, specifically targeting the violence in Sri Lanka. Statistical analysis indicated a significant reduction in violence in the targeted area during and after the experiment period.[13]

The Universe is balanced on the razor's edge of opposites. Darkness and light, life and death, order and chaos. In understanding and embracing these dualities, we find harmony. So now we need to talk about the rule of three, the boomerang effect, and karmic law and order. (I'm going with the most common rule of three, but let it be known that some magic-based cultures have come to believe in the rule of seven and others simply that whatever you put out you get back.)

Very broadly, performing magic with bad intentions may come back to you three times. The spellcasters, therefore, become the targets of their own ill intent three times what they've cast. So, if you are casting a spell to harm someone, the law of threes may strive to recreate balance. If you're in that mental state in the first place, it sounds like what you really need is a forgiveness and healing charm.

> The Law of Resonance states that you attract into your life what you resonate with. Negative wishes lower your vibrational frequency, attracting the same into your life. These lower frequencies can lead to greater inner turmoil, a lowered immune system and overall health issues. Not to mention, mean people suck.

The law of balance is a demonstration of the power of intentional thought and action. "Do unto others as you would have them do unto you" is just one of many sayings around this principle. And the rule of threes isn't literal. If you cast a spell to make an enemy lose their job, it doesn't mean you'll lose the next three jobs you get. Rather, it's all about proportions. You may lose something that's three times more important to you than your job.

Or you may be overcome with regret regarding your action. As a result, the magic you've cast has caused you three times the emotional pain you tried to inflict on others in the first place. Also, there is a demonstrated correspondence with the deeper layers of one's intentions and their feelings about an act long after it's been completed. This is the real work of Spirit and the cause and effect that comes back into manifestation. Karma is not bad in and of itself any more than a knife is. Like all tools, it's all in how it is used.

The rule of three also applies to magic performed with good intentions. The Universe will always reward those who try to spread light into the world, even if you're not always aware of this balance. To capture the most benefit of this, integrating after practice is essential. Direct the wild, residual cosmic energy of a practice to where you want it to go. When you touch Spirit, either in a ritual, meditation, or just a really good gardening session, give yourself at least 20 minutes after that sacred time to focus on your goals and intentions. This will change your life quickly and efficiently and with very little manual effort because when we touch Spirit, we are tapping into the subconscious programming of the mind. We are telling it what's important to us, what makes us happy, and what we want more of.

In our complex world, everything is of the One. Nothing is really black or white. For example, let's say someone physically attacks your friend, and the police cannot find the culprit and bring them to justice. You may want to use a spell to inflict some sort of harm to the attacker, as a way of getting some kind of justice. You might start off with a bit of dark intention out of genuine pain. It's totally understandable.

Will this spell come back threefold? After all, you are putting noble intentions behind it, to bring justice to a friend (or maybe yourself) who's been harmed, so it may stand to reason that you are exempt from any kind of backlash. Or not.

Maybe there is a better way...

THE SPOTLIGHT BOX
(ALSO KNOWN AS THE LIGHT BOX)

This ritual is a bit advanced, yet simple because you don't need a thing to pull it off. It is a powerful tool to seek justice for yourself or others. This requires self-forgiveness and the forgiveness of others to work the best but start from where you are.

1. Go someplace quiet where you can concentrate without disturbance. Relax into meditation and use the box breathing or any other wonderful breathing technique you're partial to and get into a higher brain pattern with the intention for peace and balance.

2. Take a moment to consider the things in your life you wouldn't want this light set upon. Remember the Goddess of Justice is blindfolded, universal law after all... FORGIVE yourself and ALL others. Including this attacker. (Please see Ho'oponopono later in this book.)

You DO NOT have to inventory all the things that you feel guilty about! In fact, please don't even try. You're simply finding a sacred space of grace that can only come from being in forgiveness. It doesn't even have to last. If you can only do it to cast this mental spell for a few minutes, you've done it. This is why magic is a practice.

From this grounded, humble space, you can offer yourself purely into the Spotlight Box Ritual with grace and authority.

3. Shield yourself in an *impenetrable* field of personal White Light energy. This is your auric and light body field. It's always there so it's a natural truth that you may simply need to remind yourself of if you're not used to acknowledging it. This is for your own peace of mind should you feel anxious once you link with the perpetrator.

4. Mentally/energetically find the attacker. Envision them and get a clear picture. If you know their name all the better, but if you don't, simply follow the energy from the victim back to the perpetrator. Remember this is all in your mind's eye and through the universal energy that connects us all.

5. Encase them in a mirrored box that they cannot escape and then shine the biggest, brightest, most high-wattage Universal White Light spotlight of light on them that they are so stunned and cannot even move to escape. In your mind's eye, see this spotlight follow them around everywhere they try to go if they do move. It's trained on their signature now.

6. Close that box up and seal it with love for yourself, your friend, and the moron in the box. After all, you're doing this to help the attacker find his or her own inner peace. Hurt people hurt people, and sealing the box with compassion closes the cycle with the power of the Ouroboros.

As we grow our consciousness, we become more balanced individuals less prone to judgment. Eventually, we journey what we judge, so growing into the higher wisdom to stand in truth without judgment but with compassionate action for the sake of peace, we become potent vessels for balance and order. The Universe will feel the rise in vibration and take notice. It will conspire to help you.

I witnessed the attempted murder of a neighbor once and did the Light Box Spotlight immediately after the attacker fled the scene. The box I imagined him in was so perfect and so well lit that there was nowhere for him to go. I also acted and called in the description of the car I saw him flee in into the police. What turned out to be a stranger to the victim was caught within hours. Maybe I had nothing to do with his arrest, but it gave me a healthy thing to do when I was feeling helpless. It allowed me to take my power back from fear. And maybe I did help give the situation the nudge it needed. In all of our practices, taking action when action is presented is the vehicle for change. If you're casting to find a new job but never look on the job boards, you can't say that magic has failed you.

Ultimately, nobody can control what you will do with your abilities once you learn how to leverage your Divine powers. It's entirely up to you and your discretion— the more open your heart, the more profound the changes that occur with the subtle energies.

A higher, more nuanced way to approach this wisdom is the universal law that we journey what we judge. I mentioned it before, and I suggest that you read this sentence again.

I can, without a shadow of a doubt, attest to this fascinating truth. Be it in this life or the next, you will absolutely become that which you have judged. Radical forgiveness of yourself and of everyone else is the only counter that I know to combat this possibly[14] terrifying karmic trap. Let your resistance to other's actions go. Quite frankly, it's none of your business. Even when it seems like it could be the most important thing in your life.

There is a lot in this world that really butters my biscuit, but when the flames of righteous anger flare, I care far more about not journeying that judgment than I do the reasons for my feelings or the need for justification to be pissy about it. When I find it particularly difficult to forgive and offer any kind of grace to someone who really gets under my skin, I bend time and take them back in age until they reach a point where I can see only their youthful innocence before the world conditioned them. Younger, younger, oh gosh, now they're in diapers. Yes! Here—I can forgive and do my work, sending them peace and love and strength to grow and spiritually mature. I cannot expect to feed them anger and think I will get something else in return.

If bending time sounds too outlandish for you, listen to this...

A professor from the Rabin Medical Center in Israel named Dr. Leonard Leibovici explored the effects of retroactive prayer on patients with bloodstream infections. He did the study in 2000/2001, and it involved people praying for groups who had bloodstream infections during the years 1990–1996. Considering prayer is focused intent requesting magic from one's Deity, it's a pretty amazing demonstration of the supernormal ability to bend time.

The study found that prayer reduced the length of hospital stays and the duration of fever in those who had been prayed for versus those who hadn't, five years after the fact!

There is a lot more to be said about the topic of forgiveness and grace, but I cannot state enough that it is a supernormal power to be tolerant and forgiving. Better than telepathy or flying, it is a power so worth cultivating because it will save your very life. And lifetimes of karmic trauma. I know it's a BIG ask for a lot of people. I get it. I was not always Ms. Mary Sunshine, and frankly, I used to be quite the grudge-holding, bitter bitch. I didn't know any better. In fact, I learned there was power in that toxic anger, and boy, did I cultivate it. But it crippled my life in every way imaginable, and I offer you the olive branch of peace and compassion to take and make your own.

Peace is worth the risk of not being right, not having to be right, or of not having an opinion at all.

WHAT CAN YOU DO WITH
YOUR MAGICAL POWERS?

*"The Universe conspires to help those who
dare to manifest their desires."*

PAULO COELHO, *THE ALCHEMIST*

In 1923, a scientist by the name of Alexander Fleming noticed some mold growing in an unused petri dish. He could have simply thrown it in the trash, but he noticed dying bacteria near the mold. Scientific intuition was Fleming's magical practice, and he was a man of action.

So he kept that petri dish, even though it went against safety protocols. When he looked closely at the mold, he discovered a compound that could kill pathogens that caused many diseases, like pneumonia or scarlet fever.

He discovered Penicillin, effectively saving tens of millions of lives, to this day.

Every single person in the world creates a shared reality. You contribute to this reality through your thoughts, words, and actions, and through something called the "butterfly effect."

Fleming's discovery is a great example of the butterfly effect. His strange decision not to throw away a moldy petri dish contributed to a world in which many diseases can be cured with one medicine.

The choices you make in your everyday life are important, even if you do not realize them as you are making them. They can have massive repercussions on you and the world around you. And the choices you make concerning magic are even more important.

Whenever you use magic, you are effectively changing something, be it in yourself, the people around you, or even the world as you know it. You may not be aware of it as you're doing it, but it's still happening.

And this is why everyone needs to be careful regarding how they "flap" their butterfly wings. How you choose to use your magical and Divine abilities is up to you, and nobody can force you to use them for good or ill.

But as a part of this shared reality, if one wishes to live a life of abundance, happiness, and peace, then they have the responsibility to contribute to this shared reality.

Here are a few common areas of magic we are going to study further that can be used to make the world a better place for yourself and everyone else:

PROTECTION

Since ancient times, witches and spellcasters have used magic to ward off negative energy, clear away stagnant vibrations, and keep others' bad intentions away. The highest form of magic in this regard is focusing on what you do want to see and superimposing it on what is difficult.

In a sense, magic can be used to create an invisible shield around a person. Think of it as covering someone (or something) with a pure white light that nothing can penetrate. With a frequency of harmony and peace, negativity is repelled.

Some practical examples include:

- Protect a friend who is moving to a new environment, like a foreign country
- Repel someone's negative energy (such as envy or hatred) from your or someone's aura
- Protect someone's heart from pain after a loss (break-up, death in the family)
- Protecting people dealing with disastrous events (those in the path of a hurricane, the survivors of an armed attack, etc.)
- Protecting the physical body from disease

HEAL

The physical body sends white blood cells to heal the cut on your hand. It hurts, and it takes time, but eventually, the cut is healed with its own innate form of magic. Focused intention has been shown to heal the body faster.

The mind tries to store away a painful memory, effectively protecting you from reliving it over and over. It still hurts, and it also takes time, but eventually, that painful memory doesn't haunt you anymore. But both these wounds are still there in a way because they leave a tiny imprint on your energy, your soul. These imprints never really go away unless they are truly healed.

Healing magic works at a deep, soul level to remove these imprints and free the human essence of the burdens of past wounds.

- Some practical examples of healing magic are:
- Healing a broken heart and removing emotional pain
- Freeing the mind of thoughts of sadness, depression, or anger
- Healing past childhood trauma and the effects it has caused
- Supporting the body's natural healing process in case of physical injury or disease

LOVE

To most people, love magic involves ways to make a person fall in love with someone. While yes, there are a plethora of love spells and potions out there, this is only a small part of what love magic can do and its purposes. I am not too certain that anyone can make someone else love them with a potion. At least not in my experience. However, you can evolve yourself to grow into a healthy, nurturing partner. When you tend your own garden and focus only on being an amazing partner, the butterflies will come, and when you least expect it, your perfect partner will land in your lap.

Love isn't only romantic, by nature. The goal of love magic is to send out loving energies out into the world, to change people and change the course of life. Love is one of humanity's purest emotions, a magical tool in its own right.

Here is how you can use love magic to strive for change:

- Help people forgive and free their souls of hatred and frustration
- Open people's hearts to become more understanding of others
- Rekindle the flame between lovers who have forgotten how they truly feel for each other
- Fortify the strained relationship between a parent and their child, through the love they energetically feel for each other

- Bring peace to a war-torn area by filling people's hearts and souls with the love they have for their kin

LUCK / GOOD FORTUNE

Through magic, you can send enough positive energy to create a ripple effect in anyone's destiny and change their path. Practitioners have long used their powers to bring abundance and help people get the necessary "tools" they need to become fulfilled.

Good fortune can, of course, mean helping something improve their finances or attracting the means to do it for themselves. But luck and good fortune magic can achieve a lot more:

- Helping someone become successful in an area of their life they've been struggling with, such as finding love or making friends
- Helping someone attract what they need when they need it
- Opening doors toward new opportunities
- Banishing negative events or bad luck
- Changing someone from a "lacking" mindset to an "abundant" mindset

There are many ways you can use magic to change the world, and as you continue to use it and grow your powers, the opportunities will come to you naturally.

CHANGE WHAT YOU CAN – RELEASE EVERYTHING ELSE

"Life is a series of natural and spontaneous changes. Don't resist them; that only creates sorrow. Let reality be reality. Let things flow naturally forward in whatever way they like."

LAO TZU, *TAO TE CHING*

Magic is a paradox because it is both limited and limitless. To change the outside world, we need to change our inner selves. You can perform the most elaborate ritual with all the bells and whistles, but if your inner emotional landscape is a mess, your manifestation will reflect that back.

Magic will obey the intent of the person casting the spell or performing a ritual. But that intent is determined by the person's thoughts, beliefs, and, more importantly, their emotions. So magic will obey their intent within the specific confines of those limiting beliefs and the emotional frequency of the caster will determine the potency of the spell.

For instance, if you think magic is just a "fun" activity that relaxes you, then that's exactly what magic becomes every time you cast a spell. You form an intent through the filter of the limiting belief that this is just a hobby. You don't add any Divine powers behind it.

Or maybe when casting the predominant emotion is a bitter lack of confidence. It's okay to feel that way. Confidence is built by reasoning with your mind that your hopes and dreams are scientifically possible. If there is anything that I have worked to do, it is to provide enough evidence for there to be a spark of belief in yourself and your magical ability.

Working with the subconscious programming that we all have, usually from about the age of seven years old, is like sending a coded message. Unless you figure out the code, the message itself is utterly hidden in plain sight. Your intent becomes lost in the quiet self-talk of limiting beliefs, such as:

- "This can't work"
- "This isn't real"
- "I'm not powerful enough"
- "I don't know enough about magic"
- "I don't deserve this"
- "I'm still learning"
- "I'm not worthy"
- "I'm ashamed of this"
- "I'm doing something wrong"
- "I'm not like her or him"
- "I am not enough"

Ugh. Even reading those can bring the frequency down. Can you feel it?

Essentially, the spirit of magic will obey you, to the letter, even in moments where you'd wish it wouldn't. Magic itself has no limitations. It's constantly flowing through your consciousness, and it can achieve anything. If you can dream it, you can have it. But you have to get your vibration to match.

Limitations aren't innate. They are learned by living in this world and playing by the rules that society deems important. That's actually a good thing because it means these limitations

> The heart generates an electromagnetic field about 60 times greater in amplitude than the brain's. This field can be detected several feet away from the body, influencing & interacting with the fields around them.

can be unlearned if you are willing to try. They can also be countered, balanced, and overcome while you're working on reprogramming your mind.

The person attempting to wield the magic is often limited by what lies deep in their mental programming. But our heart can help us override this. By opening your heart, you can tap more and more into the unlimited possibilities of magic, and achieve anything and everything you've ever wanted. The heart will always unlock the mind. This is a major secret that isn't so secret anymore.

Heart and mind coherence refers to a state where the heart, mind, and emotions are in harmonious alignment, leading to numerous benefits for physical, mental, and emotional health. This is one of the most powerful techniques to level up your craft. This concept is supported by research and practices from institutions like the HeartMath Institute.

Check out this excerpt from research done by the HeartMath Institute...

HEART-BRAIN COMMUNICATION

Traditionally, the study of communication pathways between the head and heart has been approached from a rather one-sided perspective, with scientists focusing primarily on the heart's responses to the brain's commands. We have learned, however, that communication between the heart and brain actually is a dynamic, ongoing, two-way dialogue, with each organ continuously influencing the other's function. Research has shown that the heart communicates to the brain in four major ways: neurologically (through the transmission of nerve impulses), biochemically (via hormones and neurotransmitters), biophysically (through pressure waves), and energetically (through electromagnetic field interactions). Communication along all these conduits significantly affects the brain's activity. Moreover, our research shows that messages the heart sends to the brain also can affect performance.[15]

Once our mind and heart become harmonized, we can reach through the boundaries of space and time to enact our conscious will. I bring all of this to you because I want you to succeed in your craft. You can have all the most difficult-to-find ingredients, perform the most elaborate of rituals to the letter, and ensure that you are doing all of this on the most potent astrological day of the year, but if your frequencies are a jumbled mess of resistance and fear, your casting will not be nearly as potent as it would just sitting in a quiet room, focusing on what you want with genuine coherence.

There are some general principles that are important to put into practice to reach heart coherence. I encourage you to learn more about this and take advantage of some of the great gurus in the field. In the meantime, here is a brief overview from the website "Humanity's Team" to get you started:

Focused Breathing

Start by sitting in a quiet space and focusing on your breath. Take slow, deep breaths, breathing in for five seconds and breathing out for another five. Practice rhythmic, focused breathing. Aim for a pace of about five to six breaths per minute. This slow, deliberate pattern of inhalation and exhalation can help you achieve coherence.

Heart-Centered Attention

While maintaining your rhythmic breathing, shift your focus to the heart area. Imagine breathing in and out through your heart. This aids in drawing your energy and attention into a heart-centered emotional state.

Activate Positive Emotions

Bring to mind a positive experience or a moment of joy. Think of a cherished memory, visualize a serene landscape, or reflect on your love for someone. Relive that emotion and allow it to fill your heart space. Positive emotions can significantly enhance your coherence level.

Consistency is Key

Just like any other practice, consistency matters. Set aside time each day to practice entering a coherent state. Daily practice can help you sustain heart coherence for extended periods.

Measure and Monitor

Wearable devices with HRV monitors can help you track your coherence levels. But keep in mind—the feeling of well-being is your best overall indicator of heart coherence[16].

UNLOCK YOUR MAGICAL ABILITIES

"You are searching for the magic key that will unlock the door to the source of power; and yet you have the key in your own hands, and you may use it the moment you learn to control your thoughts."

NAPOLEON HILL

Your magical abilities and the likelihood of achieving success are directly tied to your openness to accept the powers that lie within you.

Take a deep breath.

Let it out.

Take another.

Soften the shoulders; release them from your ears. Breathe. All the way down to your belly… let your diaphragm lift you as you roll your shoulders back and lengthen your spine.

The more you practice magic, understand how it works, and how you can leverage it, the better you will become at your craft. With gentle patience, overwrite your own limiting beliefs. Feel the power flow through you.

To begin your magical journey, you must first awaken these abilities. I hope that so far we have stoked the fires for you regardless if you are a novice or an experienced caster.

CREATE A MAGICAL MINDSET

A magical mindset helps bring more magic into your day-to-day life. It converts magic from a hobby into a way of being and thinking, effectively changing how you perceive the world around you.

To create this mindset, relax into your ever-growing belief in your light and trust yourself. Breathe into your belly and keep your neck and shoulders soft. Your belly soft. Your mind will take the cue and reach for the higher brainwaves it associates with your practice time. For instance, when we meet a new person, a non-magical mindset would likely trust only what their eyes can see. One notices the color of their eyes, what they're wearing, and how they move.

Through a magical mindset, you see more than what's in front of you. You rely on your intuition to tell you more about that person. Maybe you can see their aura. You know, without putting it into words, if you want to befriend this person or feel you need to keep your distance.

A magical mindset also involves the realization that even if some events are not in your control, how you react to these events is. In a shared reality, you cannot always avoid obstacles or pain. But you can control how you face them, and how you choose to move on from them.

So challenge yourself to think magically. It will feel counterintuitive at first if you are used to living without magic in your life, but with practice, you will be able to flip this script.

CREATE A MAGIC MIND PALACE

All magic practitioners need a safe space where they can practice their craft, which is oftentimes somewhere in their own homes (more on this later).

But as you're trying to switch mindsets, it can also help you create a magic chamber in the palace of your mind. You can visualize it as a physical room you can enter mentally and design it to your liking. Once you create it, picture yourself entering it before you cast a spell or any time you want to switch to a magical mindset. Meditate from here, in this brilliant temple in your mind.

This mental chamber is a place where you can feel comfortable with your magical thinking. Here, it will never feel "strange" or "silly" to listen to your intuition instead of facts or what is "palpable." It will never be "wrong" to believe that you have the Divine power to control your density.

With time, this mental chamber will become your reality, and you may not need this exercise anymore. Some very experienced, highly magical beings continue to use their mental temple throughout your life. It's about what works for you. Either way, it's a very powerful visualization technique that can help you connect with your magical abilities.

CREATE AN ALTAR IN YOUR HOME

Most people already have an altar in their home, which they build intuitively. Perhaps your altar is in that corner of your home where you like to read because the sun hits your book just right.

Or your altar could be your bathroom, the only place in your home where you take the time to practice self-care and apply face cream at the end of the day. I get it. Life can be crazy. No matter how hectic your world is, you can make a sacred space for yourself to retreat to.

From a spiritual perspective, the altar can support your journey towards a more magical life. Traditionally speaking, altars were considered an area of worship where people gathered to bring offerings to their Gods. They were complex and included carvings of these deities, flowers, purified water, and incense.

An altar can serve many different goals.

On a practical level, a little space in your home dedicated to your craft may serve as a daily reminder to keep going. It can help you stay committed to your new learning experience and offer a simple way to do it as you'll build it to your liking.

Your home altar does not have to be this complex. Rather, it should symbolize a safe space in your home to perform magic. Its purpose is to help you focus your energy when performing spells and rituals, and bring a sense of peace and calm.

And now, it's time to create an intentional altar, with the specific purpose of assisting your magical journey.

BUILD YOUR ALTAR

Before you get started, please note that some advanced practitioners have a very specific way they feel an altar must be prepared. This is beautiful, and I applaud and respect this. There is great wisdom in these specifics. However, this particular practice is about tapping into You. As we get more advanced, we will talk about some additional options. For now, make a space and feel good about it.

There's no time like the present to build an altar!

Here are the steps…

Choose a space - it's up to you how simple or elaborate you want the altar to be. It can be an entire spare room or a small corner on your desk. What's important is to establish it, with conviction, as your altar, the space or area dedicated to your craft.

Gather your magical tools - think of your magical journey and the type of tools that would be useful to have in your altar, such as candles, crystals, or a journal. You can also expand your altar over time, so don't stress too much about your spiritual tools just yet. By the end of this book, you'll know exactly what you want in your magical toolbox.

Arrange your altar - create your altar in a way that feels good to you. There is no right or wrong here since this is your magical safe space. Try out different placements for your tools and objects, until it feels right.

In the beginning, you can add these tools to your altar:

- Pictures or statues of deities you normally pray to
- Flowers
- Candles
- Incense
- Aromatic spice
- Plants
- Dried fruit

Endnotes

11. Murphy, Joseph M. "Black Religion and 'Black Magic': Prejudice and Projection in Images of African-Derived Religions." Religion 20, no. 4 (1990): 323-37. [https://doi.org/10.1016/0048-721x(90)90115-m].

12. McTaggart, Lynne. "Best-Selling Author, Researcher and Lecturer." Accessed August 13, 2024. [https://lynnemctaggart.com].

13. The Shift Network. "Can Your Thoughts and Intentions Heal the World as Well as Yourself?" Accessed August 13, 2024. [https://theshiftnetwork.com/course/Intention].

14. Leibovici, Leonard. "Effects of Remote, Retroactive Intercessory Prayer on Outcomes in Patients with Bloodstream Infection: Randomized Controlled Trial." *BMJ* 323, no. 7327 (2001): 1450-51. [https://doi.org/10.1136/bmj.323.7327.1450].

15. HeartMath Institute. "Science of the Heart: Exploring the Role of the Heart in Human Performance - An Overview of Research Conducted by the HeartMath Institute." Accessed August 13, 2024. [https://www.heartmath.org/research/science-of-the-heart/heart-brain-communication/].

16. Humanity's Team. "Heart Coherence: The Science and Soul of Inner Harmony." Accessed August 13, 2024. [https://www.humanitysteam.org/blog/heart-coherence-the-science-and-soul-of-inner-harmony].

DANCING WITH
THE DARKNESS

"*There may be a conflict between softminded religionists and toughminded scientists, but not between science and religion.*"

MARTIN LUTHER KING, JR.

Once upon a time, there was a chasm between science and religion. Oh, wait, that's still happening today—at least in some circles. On one side, you have the scientists in their lab coats, diligently measuring, testing, and theorizing to uncover the mysteries of the universe. On the other hand, you have spiritual leaders and religious communities who uphold traditions and offer guidance on the deeper questions within the lines they have to work with. A priest seldom talks about scientific discoveries that may contradict what is written in the holy texts. Scientists may believe all their discoveries work to prove that religion is a hoax.

At times, the two collided. Hard. Giordano Bruno, a philosopher, alchemist, and astronomer, was burned alive for his theories on the universe being infinite and his belief in reincarnation. Galileo didn't fare much better and the list of scientists persecuted for theorizing about the physical world around them runs long.

No matter if you're more spiritual or more scientific as a person, you likely have some old conditioned beliefs circulating in your head that science and spirituality are polar opposites. For centuries, it seemed like these two worlds would remain at odds. But in the last 40-50 years, a renaissance of rampantly curious scientists and researchers has brought some of the most exciting theories, studies, and profound results that have us rethinking the very fabric of reality.

It seems like we may truly be in an age of integration where science and spirituality are no longer adversaries but are seen as two sides of the same coin. The advancement of quantum physics, studies on life after death, and the far-reaching willingness to ask the big questions out in the light of day have changed the scope of virtually everything. As it took 200 years for the world to fully accept that the earth revolves around the sun (sorry, flat-earthers), it's taking some time to get the newest profound findings out to the populous, but it's happening. Places like the Institute of Noetic Science (founded by former astronaut Edgar. Mitchell), a non-profit that studies parapsychological research, allow us to break down barriers to study things many people *really* want to know about but are too afraid to ask.

It is now clear that many people who were discredited as being looney turned out to be quite truthful and accurate when they described seeing E.T.s, having near-death experiences, or things that they couldn't explain. Now, several world governments are publishing their own reports that they have been keeping under wraps this whole time. We need to have these conversations. We need to be free to celebrate the way research enriches spirituality in tangible, definable ways. The dogma of religion has little place in the conversation of spirituality. With over 45,000 denominations of Christianity alone, people clearly want to explore their relationship with the divine without being told what to think and feel. Still, from the frying pan into the fire, it seems. That's where scientific research seems to ride in with its white hat and unyielding promise to enlighten our world and prove the existence of Spirit. If we ask the right questions...

Quantum physics tells us that particles can exist in two states at once and that our very observation of them changes reality's nature. Sounds a bit like magic, doesn't it? Then there's epigenetics, which reveals that our environment and beliefs can literally rewrite our genetic code—a modern-day affirmation of ancient spiritual wisdom that our thoughts shape our reality.

In so many ways, being still and centered amid the debate of science versus magic opens the door to having a real and meaningful conversation. I think this is true of any polarity that we need to be in the presence of. Be still and know that you are God.

So, as we prepare to step into the next ritual, the Gratitude Prayer, I want to honor this sacred marriage of science and spirituality and acknowledge that they are not mutually exclusive. Together, we share in gratitude for the wisdom that comes when we embrace both the seen and the unseen so that we can understand ourselves as the known and the unknowable.

Because in the end, it's not about choosing sides. It is about finding the harmony that allows both to coexist, to enhance each other and our understanding of ourselves and the world around us. In the end, we need to have a way to convince our minds that what we wish to conjure is possible with subtle energies. Using the tools the mind needs, we tap into the place without resistance to the subconscious power. We fill our brains with resources to be more open-minded and allow the passion that is our innate witchiness to flow unbidden.

RITUAL : GRATITUDE MAGIC

I like to have a flower or a favorite crystal to offer to the altar when I practice gratitude. It's always nice to bring something to the table. We start by thanking the Universe for this magical world. By tuning to the higher frequencies of gratitude, we put ourselves in a state of healing and strength. Humility grants incredible power and cannot be faked. Surrender to all that you are grateful for and be in joy! This is a practice of heartfelt *feelings,* so there is nothing to 'do' unless you wish to write in your journal and solidify the feelings deeper into your soul.

Go to alter and read the words out loud or quietly, whichever feels more comfortable to you:

Gracious Light that guides my day,
Thank you for life in every way.
Open my mind with wisdom's light,
Fill my heart with love so bright.
Let my energy flow with your grace,
Embraced by you, in every space.
For all you've brought upon my path,
I'm grateful, and in joy I laugh.
I appreciate the abundance you have in store,
Walking with you, forevermore.
With every step, you're by my side,
Guiding me with love, as my eternal, highest guide.
So mote it be.
Thank you. Thank you. Thank you.

The physical body is a great example of something to be profoundly grateful for. It shows us how science and spirituality complement each other in perfect unison. Scientifically, one can study the human body and learn its weight, shape, how its muscles work together, and how the brain serves as the control center of all its actions.

The heart is the first organ to develop in the embryo. It sprouts like a flower to form the esophagus and the tongue. We are grown from and created to speak from the heart.

Science is all about things that can be measured, so it will do exactly that. But what happens with things that cannot be measured? The heart's emotions, the mind's musings... The human body isn't just an object; it's a person who will do lots of things in their life that cannot be so easily measured or even explained by science.

After all, how can you measure how kind a person is? How can science measure the amount of love a person feels for a friend compared to the love they feel for their child?

These are all things that cannot be measured. Science can explain them to a certain degree, but in many cases, they remain unexplainable.

Spirituality doesn't need to explain why a person shows

kindness or how much. It doesn't poke around to see exactly the amount of love one shows for their children. That's not the point of it. Instead, spirituality picks up where science leaves off and provides understanding for those things that are impossible to measure: meaning.

SCIENCE GIVES LIGHT TO MATTER. SPIRITUALITY GIVES MEANING.

You cannot use science to explain meaning, just as you cannot use spirituality to explain matter. Or, rather, you can, but the explanations would be mind-bending. That's a topic for another day.

Take soulmates, a spiritual concept. Some scientists would say that love is a chemical reaction in the brain that increases specific hormone production like dopamine. This is what leads to these feelings and explains why two people fall in love.

It's a good explanation, but it leaves out the meaning. What does it mean to fall in love? What does it mean to be in a soulmate relationship?

Spirituality provides this meaning. Soulmates may be two souls most compatible with each other, designed to live together in harmony. They recognize each other at an energetic level and pull each other like two magnets.

Science can tell you which foods you should eat to keep your physical body healthy. It can tell you how medicines affect the body and how the chemical composition is created. Each side of the coin has merit and we embrace the whole.

FINDING CENTER IN THE STORM

Just as the general realms of science and religion seem to be separate, so are politics and religion. Oh boy, what a hot topic that is. Political polarity demands that we choose sides, creating a divide among us where harmony seems impossible. It's a messed-up paradox that challenges the very principles of humanity and harmony. We cannot champion the freedom of religion by any God of compassion while also supporting policies that strip others of their human dignity. How can one fiercely fight for the life of an unborn child, whose frequency is still only a match to the mother's frequency, while completely ignoring the well-being and mental health of the sentient mother carrying that life? These contradictions expose the raw divisiveness of most religious & political discourse. When the focus is on taking sides rather than finding common ground, politics naturally becomes a battleground. When our ability to sit down and talk, to find any semblance of unity, is sacrificed, true progress is stifled.

Closer to home, there are always people around us who can jolt us out of harmonious alignment. Basically, there are people that you probably can't avoid that, just deep down, piss you off. Technically, we weren't in true alignment if some yahoo could snap us out of it. So don't blame them. The strength of your inner nature must be so strong that you can hold onto the higher frequencies of emotion no matter what.

Oh, dear—here it comes… hang on heart.

"What about all the suffering? The war and hunger and poverty? Every time I turn on my television… what about my beloved friend, spouse, or closest family member with this terrible disease? Or what about the pain I am in right now?"

First off, let me say I am so sorry. I feel the eminence of your suffering and it breaks my heart. None of us get out of this world unscathed. Despite my own inner knowing and belief in the truth of Life, the pain gets me too. I don't know why so much suffering has to suffocate us, but I wish more than anything for you and all that you cherish to have a gentle, easy, and happy life. I wish I could take all of your pain away. I come to you here to try and relieve the burden just a little bit. To hand you a tissue and sit with you while it hurts. And then, with all the power I possess, to create a momentum of peace so strong that it uplifts the whole of the world so that even one less person suffers. One more person finds peace. One more broken family can laugh at their own silliness together and take comfort in just having each other. To once again share a table, set aside their differences, and pass the potatoes.

Next, I want to say that we are not powerless to help those who are suffering. Obviously, you can give your time and money to causes that are dear to your hear. But we can also give our energy. When we combine our energy and collectively focus on something, we can impact it. Dramatically. We can use the Maharishi Effect in our favor to help stop forest fires, ease the suffering in war, and hopefully bring about long and lasting change. Imagine, as more and more people participate, the impact we can have.

At the back of this book is a link and a QR code that will take you to The Evolutionary Magic website. On there is a members only section where we will gather for change and join with others already doing the same thing. Think of what this incredible group of Sorcerers can accomplish!

Right now, though, you may need tangible help managing what's right in front of you before you melt down. As you reach for a higher rung on your frequency ladder, you might notice that anger beats despair. At least when we're angry, we've got a little fire in us. Despair can make one feel like they are under a mountain of lead weight, emotionally and physically. But there are ways that help us reset our nervous system and help us climb out. Sleeping is one way. Abraham Hicks, a fabulous teacher of the beauty of our nature, talks about using sleep to reset your mind and recalibrate emotions. They have a ton of free videos on YouTube if you are interested.

Another way to get out of the pits is chaotic movement. Ideally, listen to music without words or with only empowering words. Close your eyes and just let the body move and shake it out. This non-rhythmic dance craze works very well and has all kinds of physiological benefits. You might even wiggle yourself all the way to the happiness frequency.

The key to both techniques kind of goes without saying but I am going to say it anyway... The key is not to resume whatever it was you were doing before you needed to reset your system. Do not pick up the phone and doom scroll. Tackle a small, doable task and allow yourself a sense of accomplishment. Go for a walk, water the plants. Take one thing at a time and give yourself something to feel good about. Toss on a podcast or interview with someone mentioned in this book or about something that interests you while you clean the house. Anything that can bring you joy and make the best use of your reset.

This is just a small way to get through the day, but using these tools every day gets one through a day, a week and then a month, and eventually, things begin to get easier as time crawls on. And for the times that they don't, the more advanced practice of transmuting pain to peace can be helpful. It might sound impossible, but there are ways.

Self-approval is important to help lay the groundwork for a practice like transmutation. Accept yourself and all of your perceived faults, darkness, and angst, along with the beauty and power that is also you. Welcome all of you into your heart. By unconditionally reinforcing self-love, you train yourself to be receptive to the concept of embracing all things, regardless of your personal opinion about it. This is essential for transmuting what doesn't serve you into something that can feed your soul and assist others. Energy cannot be created nor destroyed, but we can transform it.

The more that we can release, harmonize or even marry the polarities within us, the more your world will expand. When you make peace between your warring natures, you can achieve harmony that someone else's bad mood cannot shake.

And through this harmony, you will have the necessary fuel to break down your limiting beliefs. Having both tools in your toolkit will provide you an immense ability to awaken in the world and evolve into your Highest Self. A happier Self.

Strive to embrace the duality of life— all of it. As we grow in this, we will be more at ease and more peaceful in our own being because we won't have the attachments we once did to being right or wrong. Good or bad. It just is. Then, even in the suffering, you can find a patch of peace to stay grounded on.

RITUAL : INNER CONFLICT RESOLUTION

This is a more traditional spell to make peace between the opposing sides within. It helps by giving the shadow a voice and then releasing the warring sides of your psyche. This helps alleviate some of the ups and downs in emotions you may feel and release things that plague the mind. You can adapt this spell whenever you need to resolve any type of inner conflict to give it light and then, set it free.

Here's what you'll need:

- One piece of paper and a pen
- One lit candle (Ideally black or white)
- Some incense as an offering to Agni, the Fire God
- One bowl
- Gather your supplies and light your incense.

Write down these two phrases, each on a different side of the paper:

- *This is the side of me that is grounded in the physical rules of the world.*
- *This is the side of me that is limitless and capable of miracles.*

You can also write whatever is vexing you. For example:

- *This is the side that believes I need to be a good Christian or do what I'm told.*
- *This is the side of me that wants to pursue this dire need in my soul for magic.*

The paper will represent you, with two different sides that make you whole. Once you're done writing these words down, fold the paper and drop one to two drops of candle wax on each side.

Now, recite these words:

I accept both sides.
I shall not choose one over the other.
They live in harmony.
I Am harmony.
So be it.

Carefully offer the paper as an offering to the fire. Drop it in the bowl to seal the ritual and embrace fully both sides of your nature. Watch as the spot of wax melts and then eventually allows the fire to take even that bit of paper too. Eventually, all things surrender.

*If you're not comfortable with burning the paper, that's alright! You can take it outside to bury it in the ground if you prefer. Just be sure to recite the final words as you're discarding the paper. Bury the paper with a bit of unburned incense.

II

PROCESSING

SEND THE PAIN
DOWN THE DRAIN

"Although the world is full of suffering, it
is full also of the overcoming of it."

HELEN KELLER

Pain is a tricky beast. On one hand, if you can't get through your conditioning and hidden landmines, you'll keep tripping over them. On the other, if you keep focusing on suffering, you will create more of it. Wherever your mind goes, your energy follows.

It's a balance of compassionate care, nonjudgemental and honest observation, and letting go. Personally, I am a fan of ignoring that which makes me uncomfortable, but I realize that just isn't always possible when it comes to realizing growth. There is a dichotomy in the need to focus on what brings us peace and joy to attune to the frequencies that allow the magic to flow, but we also need to look honestly at our triggers, fears, and the things that cause us the most resistance if we have any hope in dissipating them. Sometimes, being human is really tricky.

If we can look at ourselves with brutal honesty, we might not like what we see. I find that if I am holding onto righteous anger over something, it is a guiding star to something I need to get real about and clean up in my psyche. Righteous anger is the toxic sludge of the emotions. It parades its self-righteousness as morally superior and respectable, but it's a vicious wolf in sheep's clothing. Any opinion that you hold in such high regard is, by definition, not allowing you to see the other side of that coin. Opinions are tossed around like candy but they hardly mean much to anyone other than the opinion holder. Still, people feel the need to share their opinions mercilessly until they can find someone who agrees with them. As sure as we are about our stance, we still need someone to validate us. Aye yai yai.

A quote that broke through my awareness when I was in my 20's is the one from Robert A. Heinlein that said, "A skunk is better company than a person who prides himself on being 'frank'." It stuck with me because I was that person. I thought that my vision was rather superior and so I had a right to share it, whether it was invited or not. I was modeling behavior from people I thought were powerful because I wanted to be powerful too. Sometime during this same era, I also discovered that the things I judged harshly in other people I eventually emulated. I saw myself exhibiting opinions and behaviors that I used to think were hardened or cruel. It let me see from the other side that no one does anything 'wrong' in their scheme of the world. And that scheme dramatically changes based on circumstance and conditioning.

It's like the strong-willed, independent woman who judges others for being in an abusive relationship. She thinks to herself that she would *never* allow that to happen to her. She knows that she would just kick him to the curb. She is way too tough for that nonsense. Maybe just a few years after enjoying that lofty opinion of herself she finds herself madly in love and picking out dishes with the man she waited forever for. Only to find herself later down the road and the tides have changed in the worst way. Getting out isn't as easy as she imagined, and circumstances prove to be her enemy.

Anything that we are in resistance to is in direct contrast to getting what we desire. But beware; passion and enthusiasm are often masquerading self-righteousness and anxiety. Any perspective that one holds as higher or better than someone else is probably not on the right track here. Especially if one is lashing out to purposefully cause strife or pain an another's life.

You can be a millionaire and still have deep compassion and understanding for the poorest among us. You can know that war is wrong on every level but understand that the vast majority of people fighting on either side are the same in their attempt to right some perceived wrong. Eventually, people who entrench themselves in the 'rightness' of their own opinions spiral down from any level of true awakening. Spiritual maturity is stunted, and the people around them fall away. Lasting friendships wither under the strain, and they can only surround themselves with people who share their viewpoints. At least until they don't and then those relationships sour too.

We can learn our lessons now, or we can come back lifetime after lifetime until we do. Opening our hearts to consider other perspectives takes incredible courage and humility and is not for the weak. To be truly open and honest requires taking a careful inventory of our own shadows and discriminations. Then put yourself into the shoes of those you judge and walk a mile or two until you can find understanding and common ground. I recommend that we work hard to get there first before the Universe does it for us. When we become what we judge, it isn't pretty.

The Universe understands that we are all One. It is us who need to digest that concept. When we rail and yell at someone else, everything that pours from our mouth is a reflection of what is going on inside us, not them. We may as well be holding up a mirror and hollering at ourselves. One would get a lot farther if they did just that so they could stop and really hear the pain behind the words. What is really going on there? It's not about anyone else... it never is. What is coming up inside that is creating the turmoil and anger spewing out?

The next practice is one way to help unlock what we need to understand about ourselves so that we can let it go and heal. If you have any proclivity for automatic writing, you can do it consciously and see what unfolds. If that's not yet your strength, you can do the next spell-casting through your subconscious dreamwork. It doesn't mean you will always dream what you need to see, but you are using the altered state to jump-start the conversation with yourself to see what is hiding in the dark. Listen to what comes out, and with self-compassion and care, let yourself fully realize what you need to.

THE DREAM LIBRARY SPELL

Use this spell whenever you want to reveal something locked deep into your subconscious. You can do this the night before you read the following chapter so you can learn to understand why you are struggling.

For this spell, you'll only need a pen and a piece of paper.

Here are the steps:

1. Write down a question on a piece of paper. For this chapter, write "What is my deepest fear?" but feel free to write anything else you want to discover, expose and heal. The answers might surprise you.

2. Before bed, keep the paper in your hands and meditate on the question for a few minutes. Make sure you journal beforehand to clear your mind of the day that's passed and get ready for sleep. Keep the journal ready by your bed for when you feel the inspired answers come.

3. When you're ready, place the piece of paper under your pillow, snuggle in and close your eyes.

4. Imagine you're walking into a beautiful, large library, filled with thousands of books. This library is your mind, and each book is a thought-feeling or memory.

5. Picture yourself walking through this library, with your hands gently brushing over the books. One of these books contains the answer to your question.

6. Continue to picture yourself walking through this library. Move to wherever you feel guided in there and ask your consciousness to show you to where the answers are to what you need to expose to the light of day right now. What do you need to know at this time?

7. Do this until you fall asleep or until you have an answer (write it down and then continue the exercise again until sleep claims you).

When you wake up, the answer should be revealed, either in a dream or you'll intuitively know it. Wake up and start writing. Give yourself to the automatic flow.

DRIVEN WITH A MISSION AND A VISION

We have demonstrated that inside of you lies a piece of infinite, divine power that gives you the chance to control your destiny. This means the power to live a gentler, easier life has been there all along. So, if you have these capabilities, why is your life not where you want it to be?

It's perfectly natural to struggle with these questions. Rather than trying to drown them, it might be healthier to let them all out so that your spirit can be freed. Oftentimes, just looking at your conditioning in the light of day is enough to allow it to disperse. If it's something deeply ingrained or a generational thing, then effort may need to be made at every turn when it comes up. Eventually, mental muscle builds up to a full mental shift. The important thing to know is that ruminating over and over on your problems will not help you. Self-forgiveness is the balm to your soul to heal and overcome conditioned inclinations that are blocking your way of having or being what you want.

Ultimate personal accountability is difficult to reconcile with our lives when so much seems out of our control. Collective consciousness plays an important role and affects many things.

For many people, the pain and disappointment in their lives are evident because they have not connected to their divine, magical selves and, therefore, feel unable to control their destiny. In a way, this broken link is like not having magical abilities in the first place. By nurturing your spiritual side and continuing to break down your limiting beliefs, that pain can disappear because you will have the power to banish it and change your reality. Practicing and celebrating results makes a believer,

Children have an amazing ability to place themselves in the future, even if for adults, their visions can seem silly. If you ask a child what they want to be when they grow up, they will have no problems blurting out the most outlandish and creative answers. They can even change their vision from time to time because they never stop dreaming.

Until that is, they become conditioned, and suddenly, their visions for the future get more and more bound by their limiting beliefs. They go from sure-footed and strong in their centered selves to unsure and anxious about their future.

Some adults can become so wrapped up in the daily cycle of life that they have no vision whatsoever. They simply go where their path takes them, or where they feel forced into, no matter if this path nourishes their soul or not. Ask yourself—what is your vision for the future? Because not having one could explain why your life right now is not fulfilling.

A vision gives you the motivation to move forward and encourages you to take the risks you need to make your dreams come true.

Even better, a strong vision makes for stronger intent, which is the foundation of any successful spell or manifesting ritual. Perhaps, as you continue to reflect on your pain and disappointments, you will find other ways to explain them.

But no matter the reason you're in pain, you must remember a crucial message:

You do not need to hold onto this pain.

Pain is a natural part of human existence. In a way, it helps people appreciate beauty and love even more. Even so, you should not believe this pain you're feeling is your fault, or that you deserve it. You may be wholly responsible for it, true. But knowing that empowers you to change it.

Giving into these thoughts can lead you down a self-deprecating path that will not serve you well. Instead, understand that life is full of choices that you can make. You may have made ones that didn't serve you, but you are not out of the running yet. You didn't get here overnight, and you won't get out of the difficulty overnight either, but you will get out. From this moment on, you have countless opportunities to change your path and start to heal your spirit.

HEART AND SOUL HEALING POTIONS

RELEASE AND REFRESH BREW

Use these potions any time you feel emotionally drained, are dealing with difficult thoughts, troubling conditioning, or simply want to feel better.

Easy three-ingredient tea:

- Chamomile - for stress and fatigue
- Lemon balm - for anxiety
- Peppermint – for discharging negative energy

You can use them fresh if you have them, but dry herbs are also great.

/. Bring the water to a boil and pour it into your favorite mug. Try to do this with intent and not like you're making just any cup of tea!

2. Focus on it being a healing potion. Clear your thoughts gently and stay grounded by watching the water come to a boil.

3. Once it's done, add your ingredients, and let them sit for five minutes. Don't be afraid about putting too much or too little; let your instinct guide you.

4. Let the tea cool for a bit and continue to meditate. See the tea infused with golden-white light.

5. When you're ready, take three deep breaths. Feel your body cooling every time you inhale, as you're refreshed. Feel your body becoming lighter, as it's discarding its emotional baggage.

6. Then, start drinking the tea and feel your body becoming warmer every time as if you're adding love into your body. Drink in the light and let it consume your every cell. Continue until you finish the cup and say "Thank you" three times, to express gratitude.

It's a great potion to drink right before bed, but you can make it as needed. This tea is deceptively simple, but remember, it's the energy behind it that makes it magical. You are the magic. Taking the time to focus your mind and energy, become aware of your breath, and then direct it. The more you practice, the more you will feel the vital juju.

POWERFUL POTION TINCTURES WITH EASY-TO-ACQUIRE INGREDIENTS[17]

Gather the following Bach® Flower tinctures online, at a good health food store, or order a potion blended already on a site like mine, www.Healthehealers.net. Buying pre-blended potions are a lot less expensive than buying a whole bunch of individual remedies at once, and they have a little extra magic, depending on where you get it. Otherwise, the Bach® Flower remedies below are an excellent start to building your own collection. I think they should be available in every household, and I have found them incredibly helpful in maintaining a more harmonic balance when I feel amiss. They've done wonders for my fur babies too.

They are helpful for people and animals. In fact, I first learned about these gems when fostering a dog who had been through a lot. The rescue center recommended I use the Bach® Aspen and Mimulus to help ease Fido into his new surroundings. It worked so well that I studied them extensively, and I am happy beyond measure that these tinctures are so readily available to people.

I haven't found much in the way of mainstream studies that support these remedies but seeing how they assisted the animals I cared for, I was a believer before I ever tried them myself. It takes but a moment to imagine all the drudgery that our ancestors went through to gather and collect these kinds of herbs to help ease mental maladies, but they did it because they believed too. Somehow, somewhere along the line they found they worked. It is this kind of natural and wholesome holistic healing that was first dubbed witchcraft by jealous idiots that were probably just pissed they didn't know one herb from another.

Please note that these tinctures are in a brandy base. They are extremely concentrated, and you are using FREQUENCY healing with these, so it only takes a few drops.

A BACH FLOWER® REMEDY BLEND FOR DEPRESSION AND HOPELESSNESS

Remedy & Use:

Gorse – Helps hopelessness and despair - **Have Hope.** Gorse encourages the positive potential to regain the willpower to fight on, regaining faith and hope. In times when you need to find the sunshine at the end of a dark period, don't give up hope. Feel brighter despite current physical, emotional, or other worldly problems.

Mustard – Deep gloom - **Be Joyful.** Mustard encourages the positive potential to return to joy. Everyone faces occasional sudden gloomy feelings. When you are feeling down, bring joy back into your daily life.

Rock Rose – Terror and fright, useful for nightmares - **Have Courage.** Rock Rose encourages the positive potential of strong will and courage, especially in the face of emergencies. For times in your life when a sense of panic and helplessness is replaced by calm and courage.

Star of Bethlehem – Shock, loss, bereavement, trauma - **Neutralize Grief.** Star of Bethlehem neutralizes the effects of grief and encourages the positive potential of inner strength. Deal with the aftereffects of a life-altering experience. Have comfort and soothe your pain and sorrows.

Sweet Chestnut – Extreme mental anguish, when everything has been tried and there is no light left - **Be Optimistic.** Sweet Chestnut encourages the positive potential of hopefulness. Face extreme feelings of hopeless despair with a clear mind. Regain control over your daily life with peace of mind.

White Chestnut – Unwanted thoughts and mental arguments, unwanted thoughts, unable to concentrate - **Calm The Mind.** White Chestnut encourages the positive potential to find tranquility and peace of mind. Don't let those repetitive thoughts cloud your mind and get in the way of your focus. Reclaim your day and cope with the hectic world around you.

Willow – Resentment and lack of forgiveness - **Forgive & Forget.** Willow encourages the positive potential to forgive and forget past injustices and enjoy life. Combat negativity, the consequences of resentment, and regain a sense of humor when life presents shortcomings. Don't be a victim; control your own destiny.

1. Mix 5-7 drops of each in a 30 ml mixing bottle. (I won't lie, I sometimes use more, but even I know it isn't necessary.)

2. Carefully add filtered or spring water to fill up the bottle. Use a bit of brandy or apple cider vinegar for a preservative if you like, but I go through them so fast I rarely need it.

3. Tighten the bottle and turn it on its head. If you are a Reiki practitioner, now is the time to power up. Pull from your core all the love, forgiveness, and intention for this potion.

4. Tap the bottom of the bottle 77 times with all that love and light.

5. Use five to seven drops in all of your food, non-caffeinated drinks, and right under the tongue a minimum of seven times a day. You cannot overuse these. I think I hit 15 times on one crisis-filled day. Open up to the frequencies and conduct them through the body.

Please label and date all your bottles. Understand that results vary. These are powerful but NOT a quick fix. While some people do notice a difference right away, most people feel results within two to three weeks of taking them. These are subtle yet powerful remedies that are ideally used long-term as results build over time. The longer you take them, the more stable the results are. Since you will be two weeks older anyway, you may as age with the support available.

A BACH FLOWER® REMEDY POTION TINCTURE FOR ANXIETY AND STRESS

This incredible blend has been formulated with the extreme stress response in mind. Gentle, safe, and effective, give it a try and see if you come to love it as much as I do.

1. Red Chestnut is the remedy for fears that something bad is going to happen to you, your children, or family members. Red Chestnut brings back a sense of security.

2. Aspen is the remedy for fear of the unknown or a fear that something bad is going to happen, but you can't identify what it is. Aspen shines the light into the darkness and shows you there is nothing to fear. It is a wonderful anxiety stabilizer.

3. Elm helps to reduce the feeling of being overwhelmed, feeling that you have too much to do and not enough time to do it. The Elm essence can bring forth the expression of confidence, the ability to cope and a strong sense of inner reliability.

4. Rock Rose is the suggested remedy for reducing panic attacks. Rock Rose helps to restore emotional and environmental balance and is used to assist panic, stress, extreme fright or fear, and anxiety; and for promoting calmness and relaxation.

5. Cherry Plum is the remedy for soothing our bad temper, explosive anger, or the fear that you may lose control. It eases feeling like you want to hurt yourself or others.

6. Mimulus is the remedy for the fear of anything that can be identified. Fear of spiders, fear of dying, fear of heights, fear of losing your job, fear of flying, fear of a panic attack, fear of 2020... you get the picture.

7. White Chestnut is the remedy for the repetitive thoughts or worries that seem to run round and round in your head. It assists as a pattern interrupt so you can stop spinning and find center.

The instructions are the same as above. Blend them, add your water or preservative and then tip them over and tap the bottom 77 times as you send in your focus and intent for compassion and peace, happiness and calm, relaxing joy.

I hope these bring you relief and a bright space from which to refocus your light. Use them in great health.

SOUL SOOTHE OIL

For my oil enthusiasts, here is a great blend to calm the nerves and soothe the soul. I always suggest a high-grade, medicinal-quality oil because the body quickly metabolizes these through the skin. So many brands in today's market are full of synthetics and things that have no business in healing. While I personally use the Young Living brand, this isn't a commercial for them. It's what works best for me. If you have a really good, pure oil you love, go for it.

Balsam copaiba resin – This is a fabulous oil for its anti-inflammatory, analgesic, and antiseptic properties as well as its ability to help foster a connection with your community and the natural and supernatural world around you. It helps give one a sense of grounding and protection and it will open your roots for stability.

Vanilla – This delicious bit of heaven is an old staple for personal empowerment, amazing luck, calming, soothing, and nurturing the soul. It's probably found in just about every good love potion and creates a space, like a pause in time, for us to catch our breath.

Cedarwood – Cedarwood lends us confidence and personal empowerment. It soothes that one poor, frayed nerve you have left and helps repair the rest of them. It helps the neuron sheathing and promotes brain function while fostering security with a high-frequency shield ability.

Lavender – This is so often used that I must make sure I don't subconsciously discount it. I won't belabor what you probably already know. Every soothing thing that can be done for us seems to be in this versatile little flower's job description. I recommend you not to overdo it. A little goes a long way.

Hyssop – A magical powerhouse oil that I love for making radical shifts, this diamond of herbs has been used as medicine for the gallbladder, liver, and gut. It has also been used to control and command spirits, and in the Bible, it was used for exorcisms. I suspect that when illness in the bowels and liver is alleviated, the snarly grouch dealing with those issues is relieved, so that would make sense.

1. Gather your oils and use either a pipette or drop-pour bottle to blend them into a 10 mL roller bottle. I love to mix crystal chips in my roller bottles, and you can find ones where the roller is made from crystal, too. Rose quartz is always a great option for this, but feel free to run with it if a particular crystal calls to you.

Below is a suggested ratio, but if you have a special affinity (or sensitivity) for one or another, make the blend work for you. If you want it really strong, you can double the recipe.

10 Drops Copaiba – 5 Drops Vanilla – 7 Drops Cedarwood

3 Drops Lavender – 6 Drops Hyssop

2. You can add your favorite high-quality carrier oil. I use a blend, but use whatever high-quality oil that you love here.

3. Tighten the bottle, flip it over, and with all the intention of your Highest Sorceress(or), tap it 77 times on the bottom.

4. When you use it on your skin, aim for the heart, points along the meridians and wrist.

If you are sensitive to smells and incense, you can just put a little in your hair and allow the gentle whiff every so often to work your olfactory senses. Health comes through the frequency. It doesn't take a lot to work a lot.

Endnotes

17. These remedies are gentle and easy to use for anyone. However, please contact your healthcare provider for detailed information on use with any medications you may be taking. *Claims based on traditional homeopathic practice, not accepted medical evidence. Not FDA evaluated.*

WHY HAS MAGIC NOT ALREADY FIXED THE WORLD?

"We can never obtain peace in the outer world until we make peace with ourselves."

DALAI LAMA

Millions of people all over the world practice magic to some degree. If as little as half of them are truly connected to their Divine energy, then why isn't the world in a better place right now?

Are most of these individuals using their powers with selfish intent? Or achieving change at a scale too small to make a difference in the world order?

These are certainly valid questions.

And the answer might not provide much comfort at first glance: We are living in a disconnected world. We must not be near critical mass, but we can see evidence of it. This do change.

Think of a massive puzzle with billions of pieces scattered on a giant table. Maybe you have a few pieces that are put together in small numbers. These pieces, when linked, tell a story, but it's incomplete until the rest of the pieces are added.

Overall, the puzzle is disorganized. Pieces are missing, fallen under the table. The tiny pictures on them are impossible to decipher because you've lost the original picture. The original picture is the Purpose, while each piece represents every single human that walks the Earth. When disconnected from the Purpose, humans don't always demonstrate that they have much sense. We may as well be tiny bits of color and cardboard sitting on a table.

Through Sorcery and self-work, humans begin to see and participate in the bigger picture and become aware of the Purpose. They are not supposed to simply lie still on the table, waiting for someone to connect the cosmic dots. Through magic, they can pull each other closer to other pieces of the puzzle. They can become stronger and closer to the Purpose.

So, when you do magic or self-healing work, you conjure a change and create change for those around you. Now imagine how it would feel if every person in the world were doing their own healing work too. Yes, that would be delicious.

Begin with yourself. It's not selfish to take care of yourself, although you might hear a narcissist say the same thing. It's because everything external has to come from within. Don't worry about what everyone else if thinking. Be brave and keep your own counsel.

What it really means is get a good night's sleep. Drink plenty of clean, fresh water. Eat well and move the body often.

We know all this and sometimes don't know how to get all this done with our commitments. I get it. I'm right there with you some days. What works the best for me is baby steps. When I can score myself a win, I find it easier to get another one. I have also had to change my idea about what winning looks like. Again, this is between you and YOU. Not what anyone else thinks.

For example, a while back I had committed to eating better. My next day was super long, and I grabbed dinner on the go, which I ate parked in my car on a call, and then raced on to finish my appointments. When I sat down to journal, I realized that I had committed to eating healthier starting that day. It totally slipped my mind. I wish I could say that it was a whisper of a thought, but I had been completely running the most important of care for myself on autopilot, old subconscious programming that was conditioned to get something fast and easy. Shoot, now what. I could feel bad and defeated and think of how many times am I going to have to restart? Or... I could get my happy butt up off the chair and go eat something healthy. It didn't matter what. One bite of lettuce or a single bite of an apple- just one bite, and I was now in alignment and honoring my commitment.

Some people may not agree, but again – I don't give a flying broom who thinks what. I have to find coherence in my heart and mind and be in alignment with my self-honoring commitment. When I finally crashed into my pillow, I could count my blessings with a light feeling of accomplishment rather than having to sift out the guilt and forgive it.

This is another important point because if I hadn't found that alignment, that is exactly what I would have had to do. Grabbed onto all the guilt and shame of failure and ran through forgiveness practices until it was all gone. Otherwise, tomorrow would be so much harder to eat healthy again. When we don't release the gunk caused by our perceived failures, we build upon them. The structure is just mud so everything just sinks into the murk. Being even with yourself gives you a foundation to create lasting change.

SPIRITUAL DETOX WITH SUN WATER

Sun Water is amazing for raising low energy and dealing with moments where you just need to get out negative energy from your body.

All it takes is leaving out some water in the sun all day, to allow the water to capture the bright, positive, life-giving energy of the sun.

Here's what you'll need to perform this spiritual detox:

- One bowl with Sun Water (just enough to soak your hands)
- Sea salt
- One large quartz crystal
- Fresh lavender, sage, and/or palo santo (teas or oils are also good)
- Incense, whichever you prefer can help keep you relaxed. The one I use is Nag Champa

1. Take the bowl of sun water somewhere quiet and where you feel relaxed. Light your incense and add the lavender and sage.

2. Then, take the crystals in your hands and gently place them into the water. Lavender and sage have cleansing capabilities and will help pull negative energy from your essence and transfer it to the crystal.

3. Try to imagine this process as tiny dark spots leaving your body and slowly disappearing as they reach your hands. Meditate if you can, but try to keep your hands soaking for at least 20 minutes.

4. When you feel ready, take the water outside if possible, and dispose of it into the Earth, which will absorb all this negativity and transmute it to food for itself.

Repeat as necessary.

This is a good time to note—please be sure not to leave your amethyst, rose quartz, and softer minerals in the sun, or they will get bleached.

It is hard to know what we cannot see. If all the magic practitioners, meditators, and prayer warriors in the world joined together for the purpose of peace and we all only relied on our television to tell us if it were working, we would all be drowning in defeat and tossing our hands in the air saying, 'this doesn't work!'

This is why I love science so much. Because it measures and observes. We have no way of knowing if your prayers for more money were answered by you narrowly avoiding getting a $500 speeding ticket because you didn't get the ticket. If your body's electric field is still charged with lack, and you work to conjure money, you're going to manifest the lack because the charge is everything. But your magic may have stepped in to avoid *further* lack. Since there is no way of knowing these things, we have to find ways to measure what seemingly can't be measured.

Here, I look to my favorite investigative journalist again, Lynn McTaggart. This woman has led over 40 formal experiments to measure the power of intention, not to mention the tons she does informally. 36 of her formal experiments have shown significant, measurable effects.

Two of her many jaw dropping stories stand out to me the most. The first was about a very special Peace Intention Experiment that they did in Sri Lanka. This was an unwinnable war that had been going on for 25 years at the time. No one was winning, and it was an intractable war that no side would back down from. McTaggart led a Power of 8 intention group in 2008 for ten minutes a day with all her followers for 8 days. Now, when I say followers- this was her first big application to peace. She had already scored some major verifiable results with leaves, seeds, and water and was able to replicate the results. Now she wanted to try something bigger and had planned to keep it low-key. However, the Universe had something else in mind because word got out and people were excited. In the end, tens of thousands of people from over 65 countries got together online and focused on a particularly spicy area of the war in the north.

Once the 8 days was over she and Dr. Jessica Utts, the professor of statistics from the University of California at Irving, found that violence *quadrupled* during the week of their intention. Holy sage sticks, Hecate! Talk about going the wrong way.

Obviously, it totally freaked them out. Then, something remarkable happened, and the violence plummeted. It turns out that during this particular time of the experiment, the government waged and won a few decisive battles that turned around the entire course of the war. Within a few months, they regained the ground from the rebel forces, and after that, the 26-year civil war ended.[18]

Obviously, this is not concrete proof of intention-driven intervention. Science observes, records, measures, and extrapolates—rinse and repeat.

They tried it in the southern providence of Afghanistan as well. This was the most deeply violent area during the height of the war with the Taliban, and McTaggart, wanting to do something more productive than watch the replays of the horrors over the 9/11 anniversary, decided to conduct a Power of 8 Intention experiment. According to NATO statistics that were shared with her from a General in Germany, it showed that the area they focused on experienced the least level of turmoil during the period of the study.

She could also tell you about the time they seemed to lower the violence in one specifically violent neighborhood in St. Louise, Missouri, by a whipping 43%[19]. The rest of St. Louis demonstrated no change. She has plenty more trippy experiments like this to talk about, but my 2nd favorite (and one of hers) is the one that repeatedly demonstrated measurable results that give us something quantifiable to hang our mental hat on. It is the seed experiment.

She was able to demonstrate that seeds that received intention to grow and he healthy grew at a faster, stronger rate. The best example of this happened while she was in Australia doing a live event. She had her group choose a picture of a group of four sets of seeds that were with noted scientist from the University of Arizona, Dr. Gary Schwartz. They did not tell the scientists which ones, only when they started and when they finished. When the group finished, the scientists planted all four groups and when the study was unblinded, they found that the group the McTaggart audience picked had grown significantly faster. She repeated this process five times, including with a group that attended only online. Each audience varied from a hundred people to a few thousand, and every single time, they got the same outcome. This magic that was done with just a photo is profoundly inspiring.

We know from The Maharishi's Transcendental Meditation group that if we reach a critical mass of TM® practitioners, then changes can be measured. If we reach that mass, how would that change the world? Oh my gosh—these are the musings that excite me to ponder. These are the imaginings that open the door for higher group manifestations. Which means we need to each do our own work too.

If everyone was doing self-work...

- *If everyone started taking responsibility for their own lives, what kind of impact would that have on the world as a whole?*

- *If each person stopped blaming others for their problems and took responsibility for themselves, how would that affect society as a whole?*

- *If everyone just let go and released all the anger with each other and instead focused on healing themselves, what would happen then?*

I want you to think about heaven. What if our world became heaven on earth right now? Imagine yourself there. What would it be like?

Did you start thinking it would be boring? You would not be alone if you did. While many people are just craving peace with every fiber of their being, many others can only imagine the world in dichotomy. I suggest that our vision of entertainment has been strongly shaped by a war-threat consciousness that seems like they can only think in terms of heroes and villains, fighting and struggling. Anything else seems boring because we don't even have the receptors to imagine it fully. Heaven isn't boring— it's freaking heaven! It's ecstatic bliss and the kind of pure happiness that has your eyes leaking like a sieve. All happy tears. It's everyone you ever wanted to hug and being cherished by anything you ever sought for affection.

I strongly encourage you to imagine what heaven on Earth would be like for you. Using your imagination taps into your subconscious and higher energy centers and can speed manifestation by leaps and bounds. It builds receptors in the brain to start seeing more miracles in your daily life. Imagine how cool it

The pineal gland, located in the brain, is attuned to the third-eye chakra. It produces melatonin, regulating sleep, and aids in the role of spiritual inner visions and attunement to higher frequencies.

would be to sit in a chair that automatically contours to your body and moves as you adjust. To entertain the thought of the tastiest tropical fruit and make it appear in your hand. Think about the people that you love the most being free from stress and pain and able to live their dreams, enjoy their hobbies, and find new ones they never thought they could explore.

If people stopped acting like a piece of a puzzle that has no control over whether it ever connects to the whole, the world as you know it would change.

Pain will never cease to exist. Pain is part of the human experience. But working to ease yourself out of suffering is so much more doable than we first thought. I hope so far you've seen the light. It could be at a different scale than you see it now. As you grow, the sense of peace and happiness you build in yourself vibrates out into the Universe and makes the Earth a better place for all of us.

The more you practice with Spirit and the more peaceful you feel, the more you will be able to help others. When your inner peace starts to build, it becomes a force in the world.

The more you can feel peace, the easier it will be for others around you to feel peace too.

So by practicing magic, you can help to build a world where peace is the norm.

And if everyone on Earth practices magic, or at least becomes more aware of the control they have over their destiny, then together, we can all create an era of peace that lasts for generations and generations.

Magic works from the inside out. When things are going wrong in your life and you're feeling powerless, it can be hard to believe that magic will work. It's easier to believe that the world is out of control and that you're just a small piece of it.

The key is understanding how your thoughts and feelings affect everything around you and how interconnected everything is.

Ultimately, the Universe doesn't owe anyone anything. Each person is responsible for their happiness. If something good happens or bad happens, you attract it into your life because of what you think about yourself.

"As you think, so shall it be."

That has massive effects on your own journey. Now realize that, to a degree, everyone else is doing this as well. It isn't hard to imagine why our world is harsh, painful, and often in low-vibration circumstances.

The world seems to be in a bad place right now. But there is hope and not everyone needs to stay positive and be in self-control to lift us out of the mire.

THE ART & MAGIC OF CRITICAL MASS

"Magic and art share a lot of the same language. They both talk about evocation, invocation, and conjuring."

— ALAN MOORE

100TH MONKEY THEORY:

The 100th monkey theory suggests that a new behavior or idea spreads rapidly within a species once a critical number of individuals adopt it. This concept was popularized by Lyall Watson in his book *Lifetide* (1979), which described observations of Japanese macaques. Watson claimed that once a certain number of monkeys learned to wash sweet potatoes, the behavior spontaneously spread to other monkeys, even on different islands.

There have been many experiments done with varying, but remarkable results. The Maharishi Effect that we talked about before (thank you, Maharishi Mahesh Yogi) shows that a small percentage of the population of an area can lead to measurable improvement on social well-being. Their number hits at 1% when the test subjects practice Transcendental Meditation.[20] This number is very impressive but requires a focused and well-trained mind. The Maharishi Effect suggests that the square root of 1% of a population who is in focused coherence can create this measured impact. (For example, 100 practicing individuals to a mass population of 1 million.)

Another remarkable theory is Roger's Diffusion of Innovations Theory,[21] which puts critical mass at about 10-15%. Once a general population hits this mass, the adoption rate skyrockets. This theory is not reliant on a meditation practice, but simple critical mass.

These are just two of many exciting theories that show we do not need a worldwide revolution of spirit to create a worldwide effect.

Take heart that uplifting ourselves and the planet is thoroughly attainable. These studies don't take into consideration any type of Reiki or distance healing practice. So go to town with your work on loving yourself and your friends and family and know that the flower of global consciousness is blooming with your light.

This is the reason why I've created a member's only area for everyone who has read this book. We can join together and join with others who are already working to create peace in a useful and measurable way.

KINDNESS RITUAL

Begin using your magical force to change the world by helping a friend who's been going through a bad time.

Here's what you'll need:

- A picture of your friend (printed, or on your phone)
- One pen
- A piece of paper
- (Optional) One green candle

1. Sit in a comfortable place and light the green candle, if you have it. Green symbolizes nature and nurture, and it's often used to encourage kindness, which is what you will do now.

2. If you don't have a green candle, you can swap it for any green object or skip this step entirely.

3. Write your friend's details on the piece of paper:

- Their name
- Birthday
- City where they live
- Three qualities (e.g. funny, strong, loving)
- One struggle (anxiety, fear, job loss, etc.)

4. Fold the paper and place it under your friend's photo or your phone.

5. Now, look at the photo as if your friend is in the room, right now. You don't have to say anything to them but try to feel their presence.

6. Imagine sending them a positive light, like an energetic hug. Allow your love for them to span out of your body and give them a jolt of positivity, which they need right now.

7. Then, say *"I love you"* three times out loud and blow the candle to seal the ritual.

Keep the note somewhere safe, like in a book or journal, to repeat the ritual any time you want to send more kindness to your friend. If you are a Reiki practitioner, certainly enable your distance symbol along the way.

Endnotes

18. McTaggart, Lynne. "The Peace Intention Experiment." *Lynne McTaggart*. Accessed August 25, 2024. [https://lynnemctaggart.com/the-peace-intention-experiment/].

19. McTaggart, Lynne. "How to Heal with the Power of Eight® Intention: A Powerful Group Healing Exercise.Michael Sandler's Inspire Nation" YouTube video, 1:07:08. March 16, 2023. [https://www.youtube.com/watch?v=FcJEUFF37Kk&t=2483s].

20. Orme-Johnson, David W., and Michael C. Dillbeck. "The Effects of the Maharishi Technology of the Unified Field: Reduction of Crime in Washington, D.C." *Journal of Crime and Justice* 10, no. 2 (1987): 317-29.

21. Rogers, Everett M. *Diffusion of Innovations*. 1st ed. New York: Free Press, 1962.

THE REBOUND EFFECT

"*Staying positive does not mean that things will turn out okay. Rather, it is knowing that you will be okay no matter how things turn out.*"

GARTH ENNIS

DON'T STOP AT THE SCARY PART

Before the phoenix rises, it must first burn to ashes. As you continue to practice your Sorcery, your entire being will go through a transformative journey. But before you will reap the rewards, you may go through a difficult time. You've got all kinds of junk loaded in your manifestation pipeline. We all do until we fill it with conscious awareness. That stuff has to get out or be transmuted. First, check yourself and your intention against the frequency scale. If it's for the betterment of yourselves and others and hits nice and high— then pull up your bootstraps and put your blinders on to nothing else but your success. Live in the world as if you have succeeded, as best you can. Do not obsess over it; just assume the personality of it and forget about the rest so the magic can do its thing. You cannot expect a cake to bake if you keep opening the oven to check on it. In the process, all you've got is a tasty goo. It may seem like nothing has happened for a long while and then whammy – the toothpick comes out clean.

Keeping in mind that you still have to clean the kitchen of the prep process. There's really no other way to put it other than "it may seem to get worse before it gets better." I remember the first time I was introduced to the idea of creating my world the way I wanted with my thoughts, although not in so many words. I had an incredible talk with a high school teacher that I greatly respected, and I was thinking about dropping out since I was already working so much. After speaking with her, I embraced the possibility that I could be in control of my future, feeling hopeful for what felt like the first in a long time. As I drove home on cloud nine, I came crashing down hard, having found myself in a police speed trap. I received a ticket that took over a month of my measly earnings waiting tables. I concluded in all my teenage angst that "this positive thinking doesn't work" and sank back down into my pit of self-pity and depression.

What I didn't understand is that when one starts on a new path or redirects where they've already been heading, seemingly having learned a lesson, the Universe will often do a quick check to make sure they intend the change. Some would call it a test, and sure, that works. But it seems more accurate to say that the Magical Universe gives us what we focus on, which is basically what we're saying we want. When we want something new, the Universe needs to be sure that you are sure. It wants to make sure you've really assimilated the lesson.

What I needed to do was step up and say YES! I will be happy NO MATTER WHAT! Even in my desperate crying, I'm so happy that I live and here I am crying. I can only call it boo-hoo determination. I could have pulled up my big-girl pants and waited tables for that month to catch myself up easily because I had determined that my future was going to be so bright I would need shades. Maybe I would have even manifested a chunk of money to pay that ticket. We must be stronger than the first hurdle we hit. Or the first 200 even.

So much easier said than done—I know. It was many years later before I was able to really open to the shift again. It was a very difficult time too. The next time though, I was more ready for it because I had been warned and I had enough knowledge to rewire my brain when I wanted to give up. When we understand how the natural laws work, we can accommodate ourselves better.

> Walt Disney was rejected by 301 banks before he was finally funded to created Disney World.
> Colonel Sanders was rejected 1,009 times in his effort to franchise his famous chicken recipe.
> Margaret Mitchell's work Gone with the Wind was rejected by nearly 40 publishers before it went on to become a mega hit.
> These are amazing examples of Boo-Hoo Determination!

And yes, this can be a scary experience. Many people may even feel betrayed by this whole concept. If you aren't aware of this *boo-hoo determination* test from the forces of nature, it will seem like all the positive intentions, great spell work, and highest meditation in the world don't work. This is the reason why so many people quit before they see any lasting, decent results.

Decent practitioners dedicate their entire lives to perfecting their magic. They never stop learning and trying because this is the way the world was built. Knowledge is limitless. Magic is boundless. You are literally made up from this energy.

If you are "practicing," you cannot demand perfection from yourself. It's counterproductive to expect to change your life through your first spell. Your energy is probably not ready for that kind of casting. And when your heart craves that change so much, it will be disappointing when your first practices only return a fraction of what you wanted or may even seem to produce the opposite result.

It's crucial to set the right expectations from the beginning so you never get to that level of disappointment that makes you want to give up. In fact, these "failures" are the crucial moments where you must remind yourself to move forward. Grab my hand – hold on tight because you are not alone. You have a silent army behind you. Keep going.

CELTIC CORD SPELL FOR STRENGTH

Sometimes, you need to give yourself a boost in strength. Use this spell any time you need to prepare for an event that might make you anxious or fearful. The spell will help transfer strength energy from the Ailm, a Celtic symbol that represents strength and endurance. If you have mixed or Christian heritage, this symbol can be very powerful for you. If you are resistant to Christianity and this no longer represents a Celtic tie for you, please feel free to draw any symbol you wish. Make sure that it makes you feel empowered and that you fully know the meaning behind the symbol or are confident in the intention behind it. You can create a Bindrune that calls to you specifically. I am not going to go into runes, as there are far better Rune Masters than myself, but you can find some amazing texts and online work that are solely devoted to this powerful and amazing practice.

Here's what you'll need:

- Pen and piece of paper
- A red cord, long enough to wrap around your waist a few times
- Music that symbolizes "strength and power" to you

1. Gather your items and go to a quiet place. Begin by drawing the Ailm, or other power symbol on the paper. The Ailm is a circle with a cross inside pulling from all directions to a central point of power and sending out in all directions:

2. Play your strengthening music and allow your body to move freely to it. If it has words, sing them out loud and try to push away any other thoughts. Music is used effectively for chaotic meditation to shake the negative peptides from your cells.

3. Then, when you feel the altered state move through you, take the red cord in your hands. Red is the color of blood, protection, and vitality. Close your eyes and continue to dance to the music, with the cord in your hands. Focus on your intention to strengthen yourself.

If it helps, you can repeat this affirmation in your head or out loud: *"I am strong. I am amazing! I am smart and brilliant and strong!"*

4. When you're ready, wrap the cord around your wrist and tie it so it doesn't fall off. Take the Ailm you drew and place it in your pocket, on your skin, or hold it strong.

5. Continue to dance freely to your music and imagine the cord and Ailm transferring strength energy to your body. See a powerful red light take over you until you're completely covered.

6. Now say: *"The light is a shield. Nothing gets past it"* three times.

7. Release yourself gradually from the spell by slowing down your dancing and turning off the music when you're ready.

8. Keep the Ailm somewhere on you, like a wallet or pocket, and wear the cord on your wrist. They will hold up the energetic shield for as long as you need it or until it falls off naturally.

DETOX THE OLD AND KEEP GOING

If you want to get into some of the trippiest, high-ranking theories of time and space, you are living all your past (and future) experiences right now, all at the same time. We perceive it as linear, and everything you've ever been through has left a tiny mark somewhere on your soul or even physical body. Many times, severely traumatic events leave such a warble on your timeline that you may experience precognition or omens of something about to occur as you approach it in the linear space. Paying attention to these feelings can help you avoid these tragedies. I don't know why they work sometimes and not on others, but I know the happier and more relaxed we can be, the higher frequency we hold, the easier it is to hear spirit and change the future.

In the other direction, it's why your heart can still skip a beat when you remember the pure moments of joy in your life, like your first kiss of that crush you longed for, or seeing your newborn child for the first time. In a way, you get to relive these experiences every time you pull up their memories.

Of course, it's not just the joy.

Your mind, body, and spirit are marked by all the pain you've ever experienced. And no matter how hard you try to ignore their memories, you are subconsciously still living through this pain.

Past trauma and pain come forward. Think of it like a spiritual detox, during which your entire being removes everything unnecessary and damaging from its grasp. Cry it out. Pound the sand. Purge it and breathe anew again.

The challenge can be once you start your spiritual detox, you can become more aware of your past pain, even some you did not consciously register as pain. People rarely realize how much a specific event affects them unless they take the time to reflect on it.

During your spiritual detox, your pain resurfaces. The moment won't last forever, of course, and once it passes, if you truly let it go, you'll experience a sense of freedom unlike any other. But it's fair to say the journey itself, in the beginning, may not be very pleasant at times.

Think of it as a doctor cleaning out a cancer from the body. They have to get clear margins to be sure they get it all. The Universe will make sure you have clear margins so you may move on to the next level of awesomeness destined for you. It's not always a pleasant process, but it is temporary.

Sometimes it is hard, but you can prepare for it & transmute a lot of it to make the process as gentle and easy as possible. In fact, you can make it painless. When you experience these challenges and may even consider giving up your magical journey, it's critical to remember the bigger picture.

Your entire life is an infinite string of moments—because although your time in this body is limited, your energy has been around forever and will continue to be part of the whole forever.

The pain you feel right now, or will feel at any given moment, is just a small blip in your life's story. Easier said than believed, isn't it? Especially if the pain is deep and intense like for the loss of a loved one.

Pain feels all-encompassing by design. When you're in pain, you are only able to experience the "now." There is no tomorrow, as far as pain's concerned. But this pain can help you too.

It's an impossible-to-ignore signal that something is wrong. When you're in physical pain, your body is trying to get your attention, telling you to stop and analyze it to find a solution. Your body is not punishing you through pain—it's trying to save you.

There will be lessons that Spirit gives us to ensure we really, truly have chosen a higher path. Maybe you focus on abundance and health, and the Universe offers you higher pay in a job you're determined to quit for your own well-being. Maybe it seems to lay the steps out in front of you for a relationship that you're trying to quit for your own sanity. It will often supply something we have to sync deep into our commitment for better and say no to (or yes, depending on the situation) to demonstrate our level of awakened awareness for it to finally close the door on that destruction and open a new path to your new, higher focus.

Please do not be afraid of the lessons, but if you are, let me give you the highest tool I know to transmute and overcome the quagmire of past programming as gently and efficiently as possible.

THE POWER OF INTEGRATION

Meditation enhances neuroplasticity which gives the brain the ability to reorganize itself by forming new neuro connections. The continuation of alpha and theta brainwaves post-meditation is ideal for subconscious programming for health, wealth, and spiritual awakening.

After any practice, especially after meditation or something that brings you joy, be prepared to give yourself at least 20 minutes to integrate very specific focuses into your subconscious. When we touch Spirit, especially in joy, we are tapping into the subconscious programming of the mind that controls what we think, perceive, and function with. We have to consciously tell it what's important to us, what makes us happy and what we want more of to get the best results and help transmute what is waiting in the unconscious creation pipeline to manifest.

Ideally, the brain should have no more than three focuses at any given time for the purpose of programming. Pretty much anything that we could want falls into one of three categories anyway—spiritual awakening, health, or abundance. When we wish this for ourselves and for all others who wish, we additionally tap into Spirit's natural flow of Oneness and make it that much more effective.

The most potent and profound Integration practice I have found and adopted comes from Guru Dev Sri Isa Mafu and can be easily embraced by anyone sounds like this...

"I love that healthful longevity always comes to me, always, easily, constantly, unexpectedly and abundantly. I love that sustainable financial wealth comes to me always, easily, constantly, unexpectedly and abundantly. I love that spiritual awakening comes to me always, easily, constantly, unexpectedly, and abundantly. I love that I live!"

Repeat this over and over and over again while you integrate with the feelings of these thoughts and the peace, security, and joy that these manifestations will bring. Feel the feelings you will have with the completion of what you're wishing to manifest and coax your mind towards your desired outcome. Set a timer and give yourself this immeasurable gift each time you come away from Spirit, even if it's just doing a hobby you enjoy. This is also an excellent time to journal. Only be sure to write along these same lines and don't dredge up what doesn't serve you.

Turn off the TV and don't call that friend back just yet. You know the one, the one that always complains about everything. Do not expose your now incredibly impressionable senses to anything difficult if you can help it at all. If you can't, focus on the above mantra with everything you've got while you smile and nod at the world around you.

This is one of the most priceless gems I can impart for any spiritual practice.

ZOOMING OUT RITUAL

When you can't get out of your own head to really tap into Spirit or meditate and you're dealing with a problem or a pain that is too big to feel around, this ritual can help you zoom out and see it from a wider perspective. When you do this, it's much easier to face the problem and come up with a solution.

Here's what you'll need:

- One pen
- Two pieces of paper
- Some incense

/. Begin the ritual by writing down the problem or difficulty, in as mucg details as possible. Do it like you're writing a story in the first person:

"I am dealing with..."

"I have to..."

"I don't know how to..."

2. Write the story down on one page. When you're done, take the other page and write another story, this time in the third person, as if you're an all-knowing narrator.

3. The first sentence of this new story is about the problem you're experiencing. Summarize everything in just one sentence, then continue the story, writing down details about future plans that excite you, or make up an entire day of activities.

4. Then take the two stories and look at them, side by side. Realize that the long problem-story is essentially just a sentence in your life's story. You have many other things to look forward to.

5. When you're ready, burn the page with the problem-story and your incense (as a fire offering). Keep the full-perspective one close by and reread it when you need to remind yourself your problem will pass.

6. Practice your Integration every time you finish a meditation, ritual, or happy activity and purposefully guide your thoughts where you want them.

III

CHANGING

WAKING UP

"Every life has a measure of sorrow, and sometimes this is what awakens us."

STEVEN TYLER

Imagine that your mind is your theater. Your subconscious plays a variety of long-running shows. Some of them are generational classics that have been running forever. Some are current affairs. They are all still just stories, though. They change and grow with age. Some are locked on rerun, over and over, and others are whisps of scenes that float across the screen from time to time. In Some of these stories, you don't even play a starring role. Can you imagine? In your own mind, you seem to have to follow the script from others.

Waking up means that we become the directors and producers of these mind shows. You control the narrative, and you become aware of what mind movies you choose to watch.

Relax your tongue. It's all tense when you talk to yourself.

Breathe low and slow into your belly.

Let all your breath out completely.

Take another low and sssssslllllllloooooowwwww, happy breath.

Soften your jaw. Relax your shoulders down from your ears.

Drop your right ear to your right shoulder.

Breathe. Relax and stay there for a breath or two or three...

Move the fingers of your right hand to your temple and gently push your head up to center.

Breathe down into your stomach and below and above. Filling and lifting your diaphragm.

Drop your left ear to your left shoulder.

Breathe. Again. And another...

Soften the mouth, jaw, neck, shoulders deeper.

Breathe.

Slowly move your left fingertips to your temple and lift your head back to center.

Arch your shoulders together like you're squeezing a piece of fruit between them and fill the body with breath.

Relax your shoulders and find your head back to center.

Ahhhh… now isn't that better?

THE LIVING MAGIC WITHIN YOU AWAKENS

When it comes to being mindful, it sounds like the New Age movement has attached itself to so many pretenses, and not all of them are great. Maybe we've tried before and didn't even remember you had until this conversation. Ugh—do we choose to see that as a failure or lucky that we might already be reaching for the concept? Grab that hope with both hands and get back to it. It always starts (and ends) with the breath.

TEA POTION TO BANISH LIMITING BELIEFS

This potion serves to open the mind and accept that a belief stored in it is false. It will help your mind be rid of these thoughts, or any specific thought you want to stop thinking about.

What you'll need:

- Two cups of water
- One tablespoon Elderflowers
- One teaspoon Basil
- One tablespoon Nettle
- Honey to taste

1. Bring your water to a boil and start meditating on your intent to banish limiting beliefs from your mind. Add only as much water as you wish to drink fully. The amount doesn't matter.

2. Once the water boils, add your ingredients and let them infuse with the water. After it cools, pour the potion in a mug and add honey or agave (optional).

3. Chant this spell, then blow your intention into the water. Feel the power of your will move over and into the water, suffusing it with power.

Harmful thought, you cannot stay,
I cast you out, you are gone today.
With this potion's power, pure and true,
My mind restored, I start anew.

With the final drop, I shall be free,
Strong in spirit, free from thee.
Filled now with power and filled with might
I infuse my will to be realized in its greatest height.

So be it.

4. Drink every drop of this highly charged potion and submit to becoming keenly aware as the steps line up to get you where you want to go. Recognize opportunity. With each new step closer realized, continue to give great appreciation to you, your highest self, and your Divine Source.

We all live influenced by illusions and conditioning. As children, we had no say in what was poured into our minds. By the time you were seven, the foundation was laid for the scheme that you would use to view the world. For better or worse, lifetime conditioning was created. You can applaud yourself for every bit of conditioning that you chose to change. Still, there will always be a root in there somehow.

Shine the light in there and see them for what they are.

They're often the beliefs that we hold onto so strongly, they feel like truths. But they're not always true; they're just constructs of the mind. These illusions shape our entire world. They decide what's possible and what's not for us, and they hold ultimate power despite us never having given over that power.

If you believe, with every fiber of your being, that you are not powerful enough to change, you will not change. If you believe that you are not worthy of magic, it will not work for you because you will subconsciously sabotage it.

The most important thing to do right now is to become aware of the illusions that make up your reality and turn yourself from your own worst enemy into your best friend. Be patient and kind with yourself and the process.

Take a moment to reflect on the following illusions, how they affect your life, and what you can do to flip the script on them. Remember, you may not recognize these illusions as yours at first. They are often so ingrained into human consciousness that they can dictate your life from the backseat.

But with awareness comes a great power that can allow you to change.

ILLUSION ONE - THERE'S A "RIGHT" WAY TO LIVE YOUR LIFE (AND A WRONG ONE)

There's no "one size fits all" approach when it comes to creating one's desired life. The only thing that matters is what works for each person in his or her unique context, circumstance, and situation.

With a spiritual awakening, the process itself can look different from person to person. Share this book with a friend, read at the same time, and follow along with the steps, and each will get to different conclusions.

And that's okay.

Accepting that there is no "right" or "wrong" way to live, to practice magic, or to become a spiritual person frees you from a silent burden that constantly holds you back from succeeding. Stop comparing yourself. We were taught as kids to compare and contrast. Let it go. Focus on just you and stop looking for the approval or acknowledgement from others, whoever they may be.

ILLUSION TWO - THE WORLD IS DANGEROUS AND UNFORGIVING

Read the news every single day for a week, and it's impossible not to be disheartened. It's easy to believe that the world is a cold dark place.

People even ingrain this belief into their children, as a way to protect them. Somehow, if they fear the world, they will be more careful walking in it. Nothing could be farther from the truth, and this belief creates more trauma and negativity.

The world is not as dangerous as it may seem. This is a friendly Universe. There is light all around us, and as we raise our frequency on that scale of emotion, we bring ourselves to the point where we can actually see it and appreciate it. The reptilian portion of the brain may try to draw your attention to the darkness, to protect you. Like it's a little puppy or kitty, gently guide it where you want it to go.

See the good in the world just as you see the bad. Both equal forces that make up existence. One cannot exist without the other, but you can attune yourself to the light, and then the magic happens, and you will start to see light in all things. No one does anything wrong in their scheme of the world. Eventually yin and yang become the One that they are combined. As above so below. So be it.

ILLUSION THREE - BEING DIFFERENT IS SCARY OR EVIL

A lot of the time when people feel uncertain, it's because they're scared of being different from the people around them. Basic botany resulted in plenty of perfectly normal but curious and intuitive people being burned at the stake. No wonder so many of us are a little bit skittish about flying our freak flags and scaring the neighbors. There is so many who have a soulular memory of being in hiding for lifetimes. Many others of us fight to break the conditioning by being overtly different. We can't get our hair a bright enough shade of purple or our tattoos enough color.

Either way, the desire to fit in or fight the norm, can both cause one to lose sight of who we are. It can sometimes make us do things that aren't right for us just because other people are doing them too. Or maybe to shuck the normalcy of life altogether. Either way, we are exploring what makes us feel the most like ourselves, experimenting with what makes us feel safe and secure, or just looking to find our inner balance. The journey is perfect and the clearer we can hold onto our goal, the faster we get there.

One way or the other, along the process, you may find yourself living according to someone else's rules instead of your own.

Maybe the highest practice is resisting the desire to change who we are and what we want in life to fit a mold. You may want to live your passions quietly to avoid creating an atmosphere that bombards you with constant resistance. That is a beautiful way to go about it. Live your life on your internal terms. You do not have to advertise your beliefs, but you deserve to own and welcome your inner truth. Make sure that you are controlling the narrative of your mind-movie.

ILLUSION FOUR - YOU CAN'T BE HAPPY UNLESS YOU SUCCEED

People tend to view life as a competition that needs to be won. To be happy, you need to play the game and cross the finish line. Otherwise, happiness never comes.

If you want to view life as a competition, that's your right, but it's a very exhausting mentality that only justifies not being content with the present:

"Can't be happy until I get this or that…"

You can be happy while chasing after the things you want. Happiness comes from within, and it is an incredible guide in your life. By fostering your happiness first, you can better understand what goals are worth your effort and what should be discarded.

Because these days, most people want the same things: money, fame, and affections of others. There's nothing wrong with these goals, but are they right for you, specifically? Do they serve your purpose?

Or are they just another example of the limiting belief that someone else has put on you? Do you crave fame because you feel like you're not enough? The need to be known and loved is one of the most primal needs in a human being. I encourage you to foster your inner connection to Spirit deeply and to feel how incredibly loved and very known you already are before you pursue fame on the outside. Unfortunately, fame does not translate to adoration, and people often tear down what they 'love' because it becomes 'holier than thou' and hits against their own need to be known and loved.

Bottom line, happiness is not something you win. It's something you grow and the secret ingredient that will help you succeed in the end.

SEEING THE WORLD THROUGH NEW EYES

When you shine the light in the darkness of these illusions, you will see that the world is not what you thought it was.

These illusions create their own, low-vibration reality.

They make you feel weak, no matter how strong you are.

They make you silent even when you want to scream at the top of your lungs.

They lead to panic, fear, low self-worth, and depression so strong that you may think you'll never be happy ever again.

The world is a beautiful place, and you don't have to live under these illusions. When you take away these illusions, you will see that the world is not as scary as it may have seemed before.

You can see the world through new, magical eyes. The next ritual is a steppingstone to this new reality, and I highly recommend you don't skip it.

CONJURING YOUR NEW REALITY

Through this ritual, you are building your new world on paper. As it changes your mentality, this new energy will make its way outward and begin to affect the world around you as you will it.

What you'll need:

- Pen
- Red marker
- Two sheets of paper
- Matches or candle
- One bowl where you can safely allow the paper to burn
- Incense for a fire offering

1. Start by writing a limiting belief in just one phrase.

2. Write down five consequences of the limiting belief from your everyday life.

3. Take the red marker and draw a large X over the entire page.

4. Take the second sheet and flip the script of your limiting belief, and write the exact opposite. Write your freedom statements. Do the same with the five consequences, and write down what you will experience with this power infused intention.

5. Recite these words, then burn the incense and the paper with the red X to remove the limiting belief:

Limiting belief, I cast you aside,
No longer in your shadow do I hide.
From this day forth, I break your chains,
And walk a path where freedom reigns.
I carve a road where dreams are clear,
No more doubts, no more fear.
Each step I take, a stride in light,
On a journey where my truth shines bright.

So mote it be.

6. Discard the ashes outside and keep the second where you can read it every day. This is your new reality!

Example:

Limiting belief: I am not powerful.

Consequences: Magic will not work for me.

I cannot control my destiny.

I will fail at all my projects.

I do not trust myself.

Nobody will truly love me for who I am.

Flipping the script: I am strong and powerful.

Magic follows my will and brings me happiness.

Only I decide my destiny.

I succeed in everything I do.

I have faith and confidence in my abilities.

I attract amazing people effortlessly.

I am enough.

I am loved.

HEAL

"*Healing may not be so much about getting better, as about letting go of everything that isn't you—all of the expectations, all of the beliefs—and becoming who you are.*"

RACHEL NAOMI REMEN

I hope that in reading this book, you are feeling more hopeful and enthusiastic about your path. We have only scratched the surface here but we needed to scratch our mental records so they never plays the same again. Opening the door to your inner Sorcerer is a heady and electrifying thing. Of all the wisdoms and the techniques secrets I wish to share with you, none of them are as true as becoming so in love with your highest vision of what God, Spirit, and Divinity mean to you, and loving that so much, that you become what you love.

Spend whatever you can offer in a day to your practices. Be it five minutes or five hours, cherish it, savor it and have so much freaking fun with it that all you want to do is come back for more. Make whatever practice area, alter or space you have so warm and inviting to yourself that you feel the healing just looking at the space. Be at peace with yourself and do whatever it takes, baring causing any harm to anyone or anything else, to make yourself happy.

There are those out there that would say I am encouraging you not to see things for what they are or to turn a blind eye on the suffering of the world, but I am encouraging you to be so strong in your Will that when we direct our energy to that very suffering, we can change it. We infuse our peace and happiness laced power into that suffering and transmute it. This is how you practice alchemy.

But you have to be strong in your power, well seated in your surety and at peace with your inner landscape. More and more we become this. Along the way we effect incredible change. You don't have to try to fit your idea of perfection but rather embrace the concept of perfection for the sake of everything having been created by that which is perfect.

There is a Hindi prayer that expresses this beautifully,

> *"Om – Purnamadah Purnamidam Purnat purnamudachyate.*
> *Purnasya Purnamadaya Purnamevavashisyate."*

> *Om – This is Perfect. That is Perfect. If you take the*
> *Perfect from the Perfect only the Perfect remains.*

Still, it takes an incredible amount of faith to live in and accept the dichotomy of suffering in what we wish to see as perfect. This is where we surrender to grace and "Trust in the Lord with all thy heart and not lean unto thine own understanding." (Proverbs 3:5).

As we grow in our own practices the picture gets bigger and bigger. Remember that the brain is only processing that 40-50 bits per second of the 11 million bits of data it is receiving. This stands to reason that you may not be seeing the bigger picture. It's perfectly okay to just toss your hands in the air and not understand what you're seeing.

During these times, turn your gaze away for a moment and look at something beautiful. Fill your senses with it and then look back at that which is causing suffering. It will have changed and grown in the face of the beautiful entity that is now observing it.

Open your awareness to be drenched in all the higher frequencies and feelings. Get the really big feels on. Commit to finding happiness no matter what and when things look bleak, allow yourself whatever small thing makes you smile. The rest of the time, enjoy, enhance and magnify the light, love and beauty around you.

CONNECTION PRACTICE
"I AM LOVED AND HEALED"

Awaken your ability to control your own destiny and life circumstances by taking the time to connect deeply with your inner Higher Spirit Self every single day.

Each morning, when you wake, before you start to brush your teeth, look deeply into your own eyes in the mirror and tell yourself that you love yourself. Over and over again.

I love you.

Stand in the power that can only come from being grounded in Self. Reciting a mantra alone can help you awaken your powers and even send out a powerful intent into the Universe. However, you can use other magical tools to support your goals and feel powerful, such as:

- Draw the Uruz Rune, pictured here, on your wrist (or, if you prefer, where it cannot be seen) with a red or black makeup pen, a symbol of power and strength, and leave it all day.

- Drink a potion made from small amounts of St. John's wort, fennel seed, and nutmeg.

- Do a cleansing dance to remove negative emotions from your body and energy.

ACTIVATING YOUR BOUNDLESS POWERS

Your inner powers have been with you since the day your energy came into existence millennia ago. It has never been born, and it will never die. So, you were never born and you will never die. You are eternal.

Instead of "creating," you are "awakening" your magical abilities. This builds a level of awareness that will allow you to see all the things that have been hidden from you so far.

When you become aware of the magic, in a true sense, you'll feel as if you've taken off a dark pair of sunglasses and seen bright colors for the first time in ages. The world around you, meaning all that is physical and mundane, changes, because the world within you, infinite and seemingly invisible, has changed.

You'll know your Purpose. You'll see that many of the things you've been chasing after your entire life aren't that important because they do nothing to help you thrive in the true sense.

Our true self gives us the ability to experience a myriad of wonderful things:

- You'll understand that there are no "accidents" or "coincidences." Everything is intentional by design
- You'll understand that everyone is connected by the same Source, a vast and all-powerful energy capable of miracles
- You'll experience love in its pure state, for the first time in your life
- You'll become more peaceful and joyful
- You'll become more appreciative of the gifts that life has offered you, and will offer you
- You'll become more grounded and connected to the world, and your people
- You'll be able to control reality and shape it as you see fit
- You'll be able to reach for your center faster and faster after an emotional disturbance
- You'll be your true self, at last

Live in accordance with your magical self. This is the part of you that is capable of achieving all the miracles you've ever desired.

Please don't get hung up on titles or names… this is You. Your Higher Self, True Self, Magical Self, or whatever you want to call it has been waiting for you to reach out to it your entire life.

Do it every chance you get:

1. Find your true voice

You have been living bound by limiting beliefs. They have been in control, quietly deciding every move you make. They have created your ego, this part of you that keeps you chained to a life with low-vibrational events.

It's time to stop.

Take a moment to allow your true voice to emerge. Quiet your mind, and recognize the voice of your ego:

- You're not worthy
- It's too risky
- You can't do this
- You should stop
- The world is scary
- People are mean

The ego hates change, and it will try to keep it from happening by creating fear and anxiety.

Your Magical self knows no bounds. It speaks from a place of love, like that friend that always knows how to say something comforting to cheer you up. Look for that voice within yourself, and your ego will lose power. You may have to practice attuning to it if you've pushed it aside for years. It is why we call it 'awakening' since it's often slumbering from disuse.

2. Connect with nature

Let go of the noise of this busy world and reconnect with Mother Nature to ground yourself in beauty, healing energy, and peace.

You don't have to remove yourself completely from your current surroundings. Something as small as a walk through the woods, alone with nature, can help you connect with this peaceful energy.

Find the time to walk, meditate, dance, practice your craft, or do anything else for yourself in nature. You'll walk away more grounded and refreshed, every time.

3. Let go

You have things in your life that don't serve you well.

Maybe it's a friend that might try and put you down, or make you feel unworthy, but you've been friends for so long you don't know what to do about it. Oftentimes, Spirit will arrange some separation for you and very little, if any, action is required on your part. Maybe you just need to get out of the way and not engage their craziness. Remember the Heinlein quote about the skunk being better company than a frank person? Be nice and do what you can to uplift the people around you but don't hang where you will get skunked if you can help it.

Maybe you are tired profession, and you're feeling as if you're not contributing anything to the world. Start looking for something that feels rewarding to you and apply in your free time. Or work to make the people you work with now happier and more engaged. Usually, it isn't a change in work that we need; we just need to be expressive of this larger-than-life lifeforce. Embrace a hobby that brings you the fulfillment that you need and play with it often.

Maybe it's a desire coming from your ego, like becoming rich, instead of becoming abundant. Reflect on the feelings and insecurities that might be feeding them.

Take the time to identify these things and let go of them. Fill your path only with desires coming from your Magical Self that will help you unlock true fulfillment and joy in your life and in the lives of those around you.

It's not selfish or weak to let go. It's one of the hardest and bravest things you'll ever do. And before you get busy going all Elsa over your life, know that as you attune to higher frequencies, the lower ones will naturally drop away. Practice your power by being still and silent and letting them fall. If we rush to grab back a hold of the muck, the Universe will contract in its expansion for you. It wants to give you more of what you want, and allowing that which no longer serves you to fall away is every bit an act of discipline as action is. It may not always be easy, but it is always worth it.

4. Forgive

Let go of the past hurt you've experienced and forgive. You don't have to hold onto that friend that is hurting or disparaging you, but you would be wise to forgive them. Obviously, they're not well. Healthy and happy people don't hurt, manipulate, or cause those around them to shrink from their presence.

My circle had to vote someone off the island that we all loved but couldn't be around any longer. We don't miss their harsh, abusive tendencies, but we do know that they just aren't well, and forgiveness is easy and complete. Evolution of spirit and emotional intelligence allows the space for us to be healed and free from the suffering of others while still honoring them as Spirit too.

Whether it's yourself or others, forgiving frees your energy from an invisible chain. Resentment grows more and more every day, and it keeps you glued to the past.

You will not move on until you break this chain and allow love back in. So, forgive a past wrong done to you, no matter by whom, even if you don't want that person back into your life.

Forgiveness is an act of the soul and a testament to your evolving spirit.

Forgiveness is the magic used to enter the gates of heaven when the heart is weighed by the white feather.

5. Strengthen your intuition

Trust that you intuitively have all the answers. People are so used to making "calculations" when making decisions that they completely forget to listen to their inner voice.

That "gut feeling" you've had all your life but tried so hard to ignore is just the voice of your Magical Self trying to get through to you.

Listen to it.

The next time you need to make a decision, quiet the noise and look for it. Some people hear it as a whisper in their mind, while others will instinctively know the answer as if it's written into their fabric.

Either way, the answers will always come because your Magical Self will never abandon you. Put the time in to be still and hear the voice of the holy Spirit.

6. Let your heart be free

Love is your superpower, so use it. Don't put your heart in shackles anymore.

Your Magical Self wants you to love—yourself, the people around you, the things you're doing, and the entire world, even. Allow your heart to love, and this energy will flow out of you.

Self-love is the force that will allow the people and things that don't serve you a safe distance. You can lovingly redirect your energy to ensure your own serenity, and more and more the laws of attraction will create more and more loving situations.

Self-love is not something we are often taught to do, and so generally we are out of balance from the start. It's so unfamiliar to so many that we don't even know how to start without feeling completely selfish and bad about it.

Nurture yourself in every little thing and the big things will get easier and easier. Nurture those around you and feel the glow that comes from their smile. Become the person you want to be surrounded with, and you will find that is the only type of people that can surround you.

By putting love into everything you do, no matter how small, you can connect with your Magical Self more and more until it fully emerges!

7. Help others, help the world

Give back anything you can, whether it's a bit of wisdom, a comforting word, or a spell designed to take away someone's pain.

As part of this shared reality, we all have a duty to help make this world a better place. The more of this energy you send out, the more your Magical Self will make its presence known. You will live in line with your Purpose.

Be generous with your heart. Do not be self-deprecating or self-harming in giving to others—that's clearly not what we're talking to here. When your cup is full, you can fill others. Giving comes from a healed, generous nature that is not vying for attention or trying to be worthy. However, if you're giving to feel worthy, keep on going with it because you will see more and more your own goodness and grow into the space needed to give more and more fully.

8. Continue to learn

Your bond with your Magical Self is unbreakable. The moment you believe you know everything and don't need to learn more, you are already operating out of ego and programmed response. It's a clue you're out of balance with Self.

So never give up on learning. Read, experiment with new spells and rituals, and dabble in the coolest sciences to perfect your craft. Feed your curiosity in the mysteries of life. It is a lifelong effort, and so worth it!

9. Get back up

You try. You stumble. Maybe you even fall down. Thank the Goddess that we kept getting up when we were babies. Just keep getting up now, too... The baby doesn't get all pissy about falling on its hiney. It giggles and gets back up. Over and over, it gets back up, and eventually, the baby is walking and talking and borrowing the keys to the car.

Find some gratitude for the experience and get back up again. Your journey will not end unless you choose to end it. I don't want to be cliché and say that everything happens for a reason and where one door closes, another one opens, but there is truth to that. Nothing that is truly meant for you can be hijacked.

Your Magical Higher Self can help give you the strength to push forward when you hit a snag, or an all-out wall, so listen to it. Call it out and ask for advice, support, or even just love. You'll feel a positive warmth taking over your body, and the motivation to keep going.

But you need to initiate this connection. It waits patiently, hidden in plain sight so well that we've missed it for much of our lives. This whole book is about urging you to form that connection and strengthen it so that when you need it, it can strengthen you back.

10. Recharge

You're not in a race. The clock is not ticking. You have time. In fact, you have exactly the right amount of time to do everything you need to do. Use that phrase as a mantra and permeate your consciousness with it.

Take a break to recharge when you feel you need it. It's okay to skip one day of your practice if you feel tired or want to do something else. You can begin again the next day.

But if you find yourself procrastinating, use your recharge time as a bonus for time you work. Reward yourself with the things that are going to bring you more happiness.

When your body and mind tell you they need a break, listen to them and give them that break without feeling guilty. You should not become too burdened or exhausted by your spiritual journey. Or any journey for that matter. Take care of yourself.

And remember, you got this.

ENERGY CLEANSING POTION SPRAY

When life gets the best of you and you feel overcharged with negative emotions, this spray can help you discard it. You can even use it in your home to remove negative vibrations.

What you'll need:

- Sea salt
- Frankincense
- Rose oil
- Palo santo oil
- Lavender
- One glass spray bottle

1. Make moon water by filling a glass bottle or jar with water and leave it outside or next to a window to charge with the power of the moon. The next day, take the water and mix it with your ingredients (fresh or oils).

2. Add your mixture into a glass spray bottle.

You can spritz the mixture on your body or around the home to cleanse it of negative energy.

3. Every time you do, recite these words:

I Am a Divine Action of the Goddess
Here and Now, I Am Pure

GIVE

"The longest journey you will ever take is the 18 inches from your head to your heart."

ANDREW BENNETT

If you are in a place where you cannot find it in yourself to ask for something for yourself without feeling self-conscious or undeserving, pray for the world. Chant and cast and meditate and sing for peace on Earth. And when you're done, having prayed for the whole of humanity, you should be able to find the space to ask for what you need and feel worthy to receive it. Hack your mind to open your heart to receive all the blessings of Spirit.

There is always a workaround to opening the heart because that is the heart's natural state.

The wise heart tempers the mind and although we think of the brain as the most powerful, the heart has an electromagnetic field about 60 times stronger than the brain. This field extends several feet away from the body and can be measured by a special magnetometer. The frequency of the heart field changes depending on the emotional state (fueled by chemical peptides) and can actually be shown to influence others around you.

Not only is it rocking your field, but the heart also contains about 40,000 neurons and scientists often refer to it as the "heart-brain" because it communicates with the brain via several pathways. These pathways cover all the communication systems in the body including the neurological, electromagnetic, and biochemical.

This special organ acts like an endocrine gland, despite being a very special type of non-exhausting myocardium muscle. It can work involuntarily and without the fatigue every other muscle in your body would get after prolonged use. And get this: the hormones that it produces are incredibly important in regulating your blood pressure, fluid balance, and stress response. The heart works super hard to reduce the fight or flight response and help the body manage stress. It is very responsive to hormones like adrenaline and cortisol and amplifies feelings of anxiety or calm.

If the brain is the stimulus receiver, the heart is the broadcaster. Empaths are able to discern these frequencies with greater clarity and their own fields tend to harmonize with who they are around more readily. If the person is happy, fabulous! But if they are around people who aren't jiving, their own electromagnetic field attunes to that and they can feel down, depressed and exhausted.

Practicing creating heart-mind coherence can strengthen the will of the electromagnetic field of an empath's heart and attune better to the assistance of the person's own mind. If they can be powerfully minded enough, they can help diffuse a lot of the nasty electro-baggage people are carrying out there and not take it into their own body. Sometimes, it doesn't matter how strong you are mentally, if one is in the presence of extreme emotion, it can be incredibly overwhelming.

The best technique for this would be to transmute those frequencies so they pass through the body harmlessly. Transmutation is an advanced practice that requires an amazingly open heart. It requires acceptance at some level to understand the Oneness of all living things. The next book in this series will go more into this and some other, more advanced practices, but it all starts in the heart and the breath. Blending the two is potent and powerful, and despite the seemingly soft and subtle nature of the heart's power, it is far more powerful than any other system in the body.

The heart's connection to Sorcery is multifaceted, involving symbolic, physiological, and energetic components. Whether through ancient symbolism, heart-centered magic meditation, or modern scientific discoveries, the heart is recognized as a powerful center of spiritual life dating back to at least the ancient Egyptians. They weighed the heart against the white feather of Maat to determine the weight of a person's soul in the afterlife. The heart is considered the bridge between the physical and the spiritual realms, attainable through love, compassion, and spiritual growth.

Incidentally, should you find yourself on the other side of the scale from that feather, radical forgiveness is the key that will set your heart free.

SPELL TO OPEN THE HEART

Love is your superpower, so use this spell to open your heart and allow the powers of love to splash all over your reality.

What you'll need:

- Rose oil
- Rose quartz
- Pen and paper
- Red candle
- Incense
- Small knife
- Small fire-resistant bowl or container

1. Take the small knife and carve a heart on the red candle.

2. Light your incense and red candle and start looking at the flame to slowly ground yourself and relax your energy. Breathe from it and breathe into it. (Gently, without putting it out.)

3. When you're ready, write down the thing that has been weighing your heart (a break-up, a fear, a painful event, etc.). Fold the paper, take the rose quartz in your hands, and say:

> *I banish what's been written here,*
> *And free myself from all its fear.*
> *May this crystal's light combine,*
> *To fill my heart with love divine.*

4. Take the piece of paper and burn it with the flames of the candle. Once it is done, take a bit of the ashes in your hands and say this three times:

> *I am liberated, I am free,*
> *I fill myself with love—forever shall it be!*
> *Thank you!*

5. Discard the ashes outside. Your heart will continue to open more and more in the coming days. Be gentle with it and allow the unfolding to take place like a beautiful flower. Continue to nurture it every chance you get and grab the opportunities to express your love and compassion without any attachment to how it is received.

You are only responsible for yourself, and even if someone rejects your warmth, you most likely make them wonder why you are so kind to them.

HARNESSING & CONTRIBUTING TO THE ENERGY COLLECTIVE

Throughout history, witches have not always cast spells alone. They have found out pretty quickly that there is strength in numbers, and the more people focus their intent behind the same idea, the more powerful the outcome of the spell.

A witch's coven has many different purposes, and perhaps the most important was the sharing of information. You see, covens are not just a gathering of witches to draw more power for a spell. The coven becomes the family. Members share knowledge and support each other during hardships, effectively making sure each member of the group stays on their own course, to fulfill their higher purpose.

There are lots of benefits to joining a coven or creating one for yourself. But these days, that might be more difficult, since magic has been so dissociated with "regular" and "mundane" life.

But you have options, even if you don't think so. Thanks to the internet, you now have online covens, where people practicing magic from all over the world can come together.

Everyone reading this book, who grants their agreement, is already a part of our coven. Your magic mixes and merges in the river of your sisters and brothers reading this. Across all time and space. We have already looked at how this is scientifically possible.

Energy is not bound by the same physical constraints as the physical body is. A person in New York and one in the Philippines can work together, cast the same spell, at the same or different times, and their energies will work together to achieve the change they desire.

Such is the power of your magical energy.

It's not just spells in the traditional sense. If, even just for a minute, every single person in the world sends loving thoughts to a war-torn area, that place will suffer a massive change for the better.

Everyone's energy would fill that area, removing conflict, pain, and suffering from its bounds forever. Of course, imagining every single person in the world would ever come together in this way is a bit of a pipe dream.

The harsh truth is most people in the world are too disconnected from their Magical Self, or conditioned by 'truths' they've been told over and over again to know the powers they possess.

But not you.

You are now aware of what lies within you. And even if others don't, even if the people around you are hopeless about their future, you know better. You know you have a role to play here, to make the world better for yourself, and for everyone.

We have already talked about Lynne McTaggart's book *The Power of Eight,* where she gives her findings on a decade of kickass, scientifically verified experiments that demonstrate the collective power of a small group of people to bring healing and transformative changes.[22]

The power of eight is also used in the highest ashrams by the greatest Yogis in chant and ritual.

The number eight has often been a number of people who formed a coven, and the symbol of eternity within lifts all darkness into the light and continues forever and ever.

As we release a spell into the world if we do it with the highest intention for ourselves and for everyone else, we uplift it to the power of the combined energies of all, and it indeed will travel forever and ever.

When first learning about the limitless powers you have, it's easy to want to completely reshape the entire world with your first spell. Although it technically can happen, I have never seen it work that way. Yet anyway...

Magic offers limitless possibilities, but the probabilities are far from limitless. We've got some DEEP—and I mean "center of the Earth" deep—conditioning to wade through. Expect complete compliance and be astounded if the results you get aren't what you wanted. Observe it without emotionally setting anchor on it. And go in and try again. Remember Disney.

A possibility refers to what can happen. It's about what your magical powers can achieve, and how the world, as you see it, can modify its reality to serve everyone in it.

The possibilities are endless. You can change the world. You can change yourself, your friends and family. It is possible.

INCREASING THE PROBABILITY OF CHANGE

We're all ready to get together and throw a circle for change.

It's critical to stop thinking about magic the way you see it in movies. It doesn't summon the presence of a being, who ultimately decides whether to follow through on the wishes of the spell caster or not. You are that Divine Action of God. The light is within you and everyone. The universe is programed to receive your request and affirm its positive answer. If we don't actually receive what we are asking for, it usually means that we are not in a vibration that can capture it back.

Magic obeys you because it recognizes itself. Stand in the truth of your light and more and more your mind will allow you to see it. And you can influence the probability of change in a few different ways:

1. Continue to connect with your Magical Self

The stronger the connection is to the higher vibrations of giddy happiness, the more control you have over this power. It's that simple. The higher frequencies on the scale get the most miraculous results.

Fostering this ability to vibe high is a lifelong effort. You can never practice too much to attune to your higher Magical Self, or the ways in which you can leverage its presence

Once you open this door, it doesn't stay open by itself. It needs to be constantly nurtured through your practice. Remember "center of the Earth" conditioning here. It's why the more you practice, the better results you'll see when casting your light magic.

Think about what you wish to change or alter. Approach any problem you want to fix through magic logically, even if the problem is emotional by nature.

In a way, you need to dissect the issue like you're a scientist, trying to understand all the different sides of it. By doing this, you gain a deeper understanding of the perceived problem, and the solution becomes much clearer. The grander your vision and the more understanding of the circumstances in the first place, the greater your chance as peaceful success.

Look back upon the resources I use in this book. There is scientific evidence of how you can achieve greater financial wealth, a healthier body, and a greater spiritual awakening. Now that your mind can be at peace that there is an actual way, we must tend to the heart.

You might understand that you can help to stop war but catch a glimpse of the evening news and not know where to start. This is why so many forms of magic use ingredients, tools, and rituals. We tap into things that hold the frequency we're trying to achieve and use them to build a space so, if only for a minute, we can transcend our limiting beliefs and physical circumstances and give our own ray of light to the cause cleanly, purely, and with conscious awareness.

It makes your personal magic a lot more precise and effective.

2. Support your mental state

Your emotions clearly can influence the results of a spell.

It's why a lot of spells and rituals start by asking the spellcaster to relax and quiet the mind. Any runaway thought or stress isn't going to get you where you want to go.

But you should care for your mental and spiritual health in general. Anxiety, depression, anger, stress, they all dim your inner light and make your powers less potent. Without realizing it, your mind is held back by these negative emotions.

So make your mental state a priority. Seek the help of others if you need it or use your craft routinely to cleanse the mind of negative emotions. This won't just influence the potency of your magic—it will make you a happier, healthier person.

3. Find your coven—and define it

You cannot live in isolation, and you shouldn't practice your craft in isolation either. Find your tribe and seek out the support of others. Come to our online group. Tap into it when you practice by yourself by making peace and breathing with us. Go to Lynn McTaggart's website and tap into her groups.

Or your coven can be the group of friends you most like to spend time with. They can help charge your soul with love and calmness. Spending time with them strategically before you cast a complex spell could help make your magical activity more powerful.

So don't feel like you have to withdraw in order to focus on your Magical Self. Quite the opposite. Rely on those around you, whether they are physically next to you, or connected through pixels and bytes.

4. Start small and keep at it

World hunger, war, greed—these are huge issues that the world is dealing with. But they are not separated by the small, seemingly insignificant problems that occur at a smaller scale. The Butterfly Effect is the concept that is famously illustrated by the metaphor of a butterfly flapping its wings in Brazil, which could theoretically set off a chain of atmospheric events leading to a tornado in Texas. The term was popularized by meteorologist Edward Lorenz in the 1960s. Lorenz was running weather simulations and discovered that tiny variations in the starting conditions could lead to vastly different outcomes, which he described as "sensitive dependence on initial conditions."

We can resist believing that global issues live in their own separate space from us. Know that inside your own little piece of the Universe, you attune to the highest frequencies of your magic Sorceress self, help attune the whole of our planet. Every time you bring yourself to purposefully practice your magic you are getting us closer and more well-focused on the critical mass of peace. Big world problems are nothing more than the culmination of tiny issues each person on the planet is struggling with.

When you integrate that knowledge, you will know you need only start small when changing the world. You'll know how big of a difference you can make when you change your own perspective. It could unleash a domino effect of change. You are the person you need to change. And your spell just has to be powerful enough to push that first domino.

Have faith and keep a journal of all the wonderful things that happen throughout the day. Write down every good thing you love in your life and every gratitude you have and watch them flower into a bigger and bigger garden. Know that you are not alone. You are always connected to a stunning mosaic of creation that exists to celebrate you. Focus on your breath. Ground the body and make it soft and pliable. Release the mind and hear only the breath moving in and out. Listen to the sound. The sound, and then the space between—that's where you will find what You are.

TIME BENDING GROUP MEDITATION FOR PEACE

Together, you and all the readers of this book, along with those I have taught and practiced The Mysteries, we each presence ourselves in one spirit-bound location. We are breathing together here and now with you.

Read through this a couple of times and then relax into the actual practice.

Use your favorite breathing technique and allow your body to relax. Allow the whispers of thought to pass and focus your eyes gently on the third eye. Trigger that delicious part of yourself that enjoys the light and free happiness that comes from dancing with Spirit.

We are going to work in the present, and we are going to use the light force of all those who have or will magic in this place occupy here together in this intention. We will give our strength to the call of the highest among us. We breathe in the circle of all that ever was and all that will be here and now within ourselves.

For we are proven to be One. To this we bow our heads and hearts together.

We call from the One that we are to all who are making decisions that affect others.

Peace to you. Compassion and mercy and peace to you.

We forgive you. You are forgiven. Start with Now. Here and now, you are peace and you live to serve the highest among us in peace and compassion, and mercy and goodness you give to the lowest among us. Peace to you. We give our peace to you. The more we give, the more we have, and peace flows to all living beings here and now and in every breath we take.

We reach out to you from the calling of our soul—take our love. We are filled with love for you, and we see you more and more healing and giving life, love and understanding.

You are the forgiven one. You are healing, healed light for others, and we support you with our hearts and our light.

See the silos that are to hold bombs being empty. All over the world, nothing but empty silos and happy hearts. Peace and freedom and relief for those who would have been forced to war. See them embracing their families. Celebrating their freedom.

See the children in the safe and protected streets smiling and happy. A sea of people's faces smiling and happy. All over the world, everywhere and every place, smiling, relieved and happy faces.

See the oceans, cool and calm and clean and clear. Happy critters diving in its crystalline depths.

Don't linger so long that you start thinking of the problems we are meant to solve. This isn't the time or place for that. You are not alone, and all you need to do is close your eyes and smile from the center of your chest. Take the hand of the spirit of the person next to you and once again...

We call from the One that we are to all who are making decisions that affect others.

Peace to You. Compassion and mercy and peace to you.

We forgive you. You are forgiven. Start with Now. Here and now, you are peace, and you live to serve the highest among us in peace and compassion, and mercy and goodness you give to the lowest among us. Peace to you. We give our peace to you. The more we give, the more we have, and peace flows to all living beings here and now and in every breath we take.

We reach out to you from the calling of our soul—take our love. We are filled with love for you, and we see you more and more healing and giving life and love and understanding.

You are the forgiven one. You are healing, healed light for others and we support you with our hearts and our light.

Once you are done seeing all the smiling happy faces of the planet... relax into Integration and practice your mantras of reconditioning for the next 20 minutes:

I always love that I am so happy! I always love that I am healthy and long of life. I always love that I am spiritually awakened. I am so happy. I always love that financial abundance comes to me always, easily, constantly and joyfully. Thank you! Thank you! Thank you!

Endnotes

22. McTaggart, Lynne. *The Power of Eight: Harnessing the Miraculous Energies of a Small Group to Heal Others, Your Life, and the World.* New York: Atria Books, 2017.

IV

DOING

"Start by doing what's necessary;
then do what's possible; and suddenly you
are doing the impossible."

SAINT FRANCIS OF ASSISI

Up until this point, I've already offered you a lot of sciencey-spirit stuff to think about and plenty of rituals to try. It's perfectly okay if you haven't done everything up until this point. Work at your own pace; however, push yourself where you can. You cannot get different results by doing the same old things. Malcolm Gladwell would say that one requires 10,000 hours of practice to become a Master.

In the next few pages, you'll find some easy spells you can use in your practice to manifest love, health, and abundance while you work on your mindscape. Feel free to add these spells in your personal grimoires and journals which you can develop over time with new rituals, spells, and words of wisdom from your daily musings and other sources.

I recommend reading the very basic practices in this next section as ways to start jogging your old conditioning free. If you have read anything in this book, you might think that the next section is a bit of a joke. In a way it is. They all are! They are jokes on us because all we really need is clear emotional thought to manifest our desires. But until our Sorcery is of that high mage caliber, some of us might want a little extra help. So, play with the rituals and activities that follow and use them as a starting point to perfect your own flavor of the spell.

Apply the techniques to these rituals. Use your breath, use your focus, and use your intention because all the flowery practice below is only a way for you to do that without distraction.

Make these your spells. Journal what you do and what you observe in the days that follow and track your successes. See what worked the best for you and what feels the best and build on that.

Remember that there are amazing resources out there to help grow you on your frequency scale. For example, when it comes to relationships, I HIGHLY recommend reading just about anything from Alison Armstrong.[23] She has her own community online, and I cannot say enough how this woman supports the world with her insights on human relationships. If you want to attract or keep a relationship, check out this queen of love magic.

HOUSEKEEPING NOTE ON FIRE MAGIC

While most candle spells require you to let the candle burn, if you choose to put it out, please do not use your lifeforce breath to do so. Let your breath give only life. Clapping out candles or snuffing them with a snuffer is a higher way to perform fire magic. Clapping out candles is also a nicer way to share birthday cake without all the spit flying so win/ win.

LOVE MAGIC

SPELL TO ATTRACT THE PERFECT LOVER

What you'll need:

- First and foremost, to be a reflection of who you want to attract
- Handful of rose petals
- One rose quartz
- One teaspoon of lavender (fresh, dried, or oils)
- One teaspoon of cinnamon
- One square piece of red fabric
- One piece of pink ribbon or string
- Space in your journal or grimoire to write down what you seek in a partner

When to perform this spell: Waxing Moon

What you need to do:

- At night during the Waxing Moon, gather all your ingredients
- Place the red fabric on the floor and slowly add each ingredient in the middle, with purpose
- Gather each corner of the fabric and tie them together with your pink string, to create a pouch
- Bring the pouch to your heart and recite this incantation:

I sit here pure, with heart laid bare,
Bring me the love that's meant to share.
Bring me the one who's meant to be,
The lover written in destiny.
I strive to be all that I seek,
Nurturing both strong and weak.
With loving eyes, I make my way,
Preparing for love that's here to stay.
Thank you, thank you, endlessly,
For the love that's coming, meant for me.

- Write down the traits that you want in your partner. Next, write down three ways that you demonstrate those traits yourself. If you can't think of three, write down ways you will nurture that trait in yourself to be the partner you wish to attract

- Continue to keep the pouch to your heart, and imagine a red, magnetic light coming from it, attracting your lover

- Keep the pouch on your person, or sleep with it under the pillow

- Continue to review the traits that you want, are and are becoming

- Journal how you're strengthening yourself in these ways

- When your lover arrives, hang the pouch from a tree branch somewhere near your home and practice being the partner you want your partner to be. Allow the mirror of kindness and love to enrapture you in your new relationship

LOVE POTION (WITH RED WINE)

What you'll need:

- One pink candle
- A few pinches of nutmeg, basil, and lavender
- One cup of red wine (if you don't consume alcohol, use grape juice)
- One saucepan
- One small knife

What you need to do:

- Take the pink candle and the knife, and carve two hearts interlocking, like so:

- Light the candle, place it near your stove, and recite:

As this candle burns bright,
So does his/her love.
Bring her/him to me,
For we are meant to be.

- Put your ingredients in the saucepan, then pour the red wine on top
- Let the mixture boil, and turn off the heat
- Pour your potion in your favorite mug, then chant this a few times while it's cooling:

I give true love to you. Bring true love to me.

- When it's ready, drink the potion to the last drop, envisioning all the ways you are what you want to attract and how you can give everything that you wish to receive
- Allow it to magnetize your energy to attract your manifest love

TO CREATE NEW FRIENDSHIPS

What you'll need:

- One yellow candle
- Rose quartz
- Bergamot or Sacred Frankincense oil

What you need to do:

- Carve your name on the yellow candle and add a few drops of your oil on it to anoint it
- Light the candle and take the rose quartz in your hands
- Clear your mind of distracting thoughts and focus on the idea and feeling of friendship while you gaze at the flame
- Think of what it means to you, what it makes you feel, and what role a new friend may have in your life
- If you are thinking of a specific person, visualize your friendship together
- When you're ready, chant this three times:

I am ready for new friendships.
I am open to new beginnings.
I accept all the love and kindness new friendships provide.
I am a good and wonderful friend.
I attract goodness and kindness and I give and receive.
Nothing but the very best.

- You can also chant the name of a specific person three times if you have someone in mind
- Once you've watched the flame burn all the way while envisioning what friendship feels and looks like, set to carry the rose quartz in your pocket until the new friendship forms
- You can also place the rose quartz on your altar to do its job from there
- When you see an opportunity, take it and invite your new friend to coffee or for a walk

SPELL TO HEAL A BROKEN HEART

What you'll need:

- Nine red candles
- A photo of the person whose broken heart you want to heal. You can also write their name on a piece of paper

What you need to do:

- Put all the candles in a circle, with the photo in the center
- Light each candle slowly, saying these words:

Cleansing flames, burn bright
And release heartbreak from my sight.

- You'll repeat these words nine times, for each candle
- Focus on forgiveness of yourself and the other person (remember the trick to take them to a place of youth, or even childhood if that is the only way you can see them in a state you can practice forgiveness)
- When you're done, let the candles completely burn out
- When all the candles are burned out, the spell is complete

SPELL TO HEAL A BROKEN HEART II
(GRAPHIC & DARK CONTENT WARNING)

Okay, so maybe you're a little more broken than a fire ritual can heal. I get it. Sometimes things are bad. Really bad. The following is a technique I only used only once on a 'friend' who had betrayed me in such a financially and emotionally brutal way, that I had no idea how to pick up the pieces. While I'm not proud of it, it gave my mind the space it needed to see the 'perpetrator' suffer enough that my heart was finally allowed the space it had to have to grieve for once and for all. Finally, after this technique, I was able to forgive. Time does help heal all wounds, but this helped me to get free from my prison mind and get past the pain so I could function again.

Sit in your magic space or outside where you won't be disturbed. This can be intense, and I'm pretty sure I screamed out loud so have a pillow handy if you need to muffle sound.

Picture the person that hurt you. This person that made you suffer. Now grab them by the scruff of their soul and fly up and pin their soul to the surface of the sun. That huge ball of flame that gives us life and itself is alive. Pin them to it where they cannot escape.

Watch as their skin and muscles burn from their body. Watch them scream and writhe in agony as they fry. Watch them as their bones melt and their pain is so complete that pure agony is all they are.

Then, because you've pinned their soul, their 'body' immediately reforms, and they go through it all over again. And again and again, until you have seen them suffer enough to cool the fire within your cells that won't let you think straight.

Give your reptilian mind what it needs to get past the trauma so you can move to forgiveness of them and yourself, at any age you need to go back to. Because hurt people hurt people. And your conditioning allowed the space that made you vulnerable to them in the first place. You've got to forgive. You have suffered. Now they have suffered—immensely!

Remember all that we have learned about the power of the mind. If you can see it, on some level it is done. Watch them endure what no creature should ever have to until you've had your fill. Then get to where you can transmute it with forgiveness of yourself and of them and burn through the pain that is smothering you. When you're ready, release their soul, thereby releasing your soul, and let them flutter away to heal. Or see them being absorbed by the One where they cannot hurt anyone else.

From this practice, the only Integration that may be possible is something like…

I am peace. There is peace. I give peace. I receive peace.
I am forgiven. I forgive.

Give yourself peace and forgiveness and healing and love and kindness and more peace for the 20-minute Integration and let your soul (and theirs) heal.

This is only for those times when you cannot think around your anger and suffering. You have been hurt so badly that you cannot find your way to heal. Practice this with caution. Neither of you will ever be the same.

Endnotes

23. Alison Armstrong. "Begin Your Journey." Accessed August 13, 2024. [https://www.alisonarmstrong.com]

ABUNDANCE MAGIC

"Financial abundance is a natural byproduct of aligning with your true purpose and passion."

JACK CANFIELD

MOON SPELL TO ATTRACT MONEY

What you'll need:

- One green candle
- Lemongrass or Patchouli oil

When to perform it: During the full moon

What you need to do:

- Take the candle where you can sit in the moonlight and dress it with the oil by adding just a drop or two
- Light the candle and look closely at the flame
- Quiet the mind of distracting thoughts and focus on what you want: money
- Do you have a certain amount you want? See it. Visualize it in your hands, the way it smells and feels
- Take three deep breaths in that feeling, and repeat this short incantation:

My path is weighed by
[why you need the money, such as an expensive medical bill]
To be free of this, I seek the will.
I cast my fears into the flame,
With pure intent, I stake my claim.
Abundance flows, both near and far,
Prosperity shines like a guiding star.
$____ is mine, with ease it comes,
In constant streams, my wealth hums.

- Let your candle burn and bask in the moonlight, charging yourself with abundance
- Let its light connect with yours, as you attract money and wealth
- As the candle completes its burn, and as often as you can throughout the process, empower the spell by saying "thank you" three times with incredible gratitude and feeling

SPELL TO INVITE PROSPERITY

What you'll need:

- One green candle
- Bill, coin, or another object that symbolizes money and prosperity (such as a credit card)
- Paper and pen

What you need to do:

- Gather your materials and think about what you want
- Define prosperity before you begin the spell. The more specific you are, the better. For instance, don't just hope for "new opportunities" but hope for "a new job offer that will pay me 20% more" for example.
- Write down your goal on the piece of paper
- Light the green candle, place the prosperity object next to it, and hold the paper in your hand
- Visualize your life after you get what you want. If it's a new job, picture yourself at the new office, being happy with the work and getting your first paycheck
- When you're ready, burn the piece of paper and say this three times:

Thank you for this abundant and prosperous path!

- Once the paper burns, put out the candle with a clap of your hands or use a snuffer and give thanks.

SPELL TO ACHIEVE BUSINESS SUCCESS

What you'll need:

- Handful of basil seeds
- One flower pot
- Soil
- Eight pennies (eight symbolizes that eternal success)

What you need to do:

- Take the pot and fill half of it with soil
- Take the eight pennies and place them in a circle, in a clockwise motion
- Cover the pennies with more soil, then add the basil seeds
- Recite this chant:

> *Basil, penny, soil; unite with my will and heart.*
> *My business flourishes as these seeds sprout and grow.*
> *As I will it, it shall be so.*

- Continue to water the plant and care for it, so it grows strong
- It is now connected to your business. As it prospers, so will your business
- If and when it should pass, the roots have released their hold on your business to fly on its own.
- Use the dried leaves for future abundance rites

If you're not the greatest of green thumbs, you can use a starter plant and adjust as needed.

INCENSE TO CREATE ABUNDANT
ENERGY IN THE HOME

What you'll need:

- One part ground nutmeg
- Two parts ground cinnamon
- One part dried myrtle
- One part benzoin
- Other elements you want, depending on what type of abundance you want to attract

What to do:

- Bring all the ingredients together and store them in a closed bottle or jar
- When you need to fill your home with abundant energy, burn around a teaspoon at a time
- Try to let the fumes get in your entire home. You can carry the incense through the room if necessary
- As you do this, you can recite an affirmation that attracts abundance, such as *"Prosperity clings to me effortlessly and easily."*

POTION TEA TO UNLOCK NEW OPPORTUNITIES

What you'll need:

- Garden sage, for cleansing
- Basil, for abundance
- Lavender, for joy
- Cinnamon, for success
- Rosemary, for clarity

What you need to do:

- Take a pot, add water, and bring it to a boil. Let it simmer
- Add each ingredient in the water in this exact order and repeat these words:

I add thee, garden sage, to absorb and remove
all my low vibrations and bad luck
I add thee, basil, to attract prosperity
I add thee, lavender, to fill my heart with joy
I add thee, cinnamon, to foster success and accomplishment.
Finally, thee rosemary, bring clarity to my path and show me
The open door which I cannot yet see.

- Stir the brew in a clockwise motion
- Let it sit for a few minutes, then pour yourself a cup
- Dispose of the used herbs by your front door
- The potion will help you see a new opportunity soon.

HEALING MAGIC

"What you think you create.
What you feel you attract.
And what you imagine you become"

BUDDHA

HEALING SOMEONE WHO IS SICK

What you'll need:

- One white candle
- One pinecone
- Paper and pen
- Piece of green thread

What you need to do:

- Write the name of the person you want to heal and their illness (physical or emotional)
- Light the white candle
- Take the paper and wrap it around the pinecone. Carefully tie it with the green thread
- Recite this incantation:

Hear these words, hear my plea
On behalf of [Name] to heal their [illness], I come to thee.
Fill them only with peace and joy
Walk by their side during this fight
And use your infinite powers to take away their sickness.
Thank you. Thank you. Thank you.

- Let the candle burn out and keep the pinecone in your home, or preferably give it to the person who is sick. Its energy will support their healing process.

HEALING II

Bring your healing concern to a group who can help you. Come to CLBiggs.com and post your intention for others to work with you. Add it to a prayer temple or get your coven together to send energy for at least ten minutes a day over 8 days.

WATER SPELL TO REMOVE NEGATIVE ENERGY

What you'll need:

- Pen or marker
- Rice paper
- A bowl of sun-charged water

What you need to do:

- Take the pen and rice paper and write these words on it:

I come to you in time of need.
Anoint me with strength and light today, tomorrow, and always.
Grace me with love, joy, and peace,
Fill my mind with wisdom and clarity,
Remove that which does not serve me,
Transmute it that I am free.

- Put the rice paper in the sun water bowl and let it dissolve while you feel it pull the negative energy from you to the water through the paper
- Once it disappears, give the water to the Earth or your favorite plant, and visualize negative energy leaving you and being transmuted by the Earth. The same kind of sticky energy that drains a human can nourish plants. Let what no longer serves you be food for something else

You can also write any other spell you want on rice paper, to remove things that do not serve you, such as a hard challenge, negative emotion, and more.

MIND-CLEANSING BATH

What you'll need:

- Your favorite relaxing music
- Rosemary
- Basil
- Orange peels
- Rose petals
- Lavender
- If you use herbs, peels, and petals, wrap them in a tea bag or cheesecloth
- If you prefer, you can use oils, but be mindful of the slippery cleanup

What you need to do:

- Fill up a bath and add all your ingredients
- Play your relaxing music, and get in the water
- Sit for 10 minutes at least, and repeat this mantra over and over:

    I release myself from all that no longer serves me.
    I am free. I am happy. I am at peace.

- You can continue to meditate, or just focus on the relaxing music
- When you're ready, remove the plants from the bath, and drain the water

- It will carry away all unwanted thoughts from your mind, and help you gain clarity and focus
- Should the echo of these thoughts reemerge later, gently remind them they are a ghost of what slid down the drain and direct your mind to more pleasant thoughts

MIND-BODY REALIGNMENT

What you'll need:

- A quiet place where you can lie down

What you need to do:

- Lie down on your back, face up, and keep your arms and legs straight
- Close your eyes and bring your attention to each part of your body at a time
- Begin with your toes, then slowly go up
- Try not to move your body during this ritual. The goal is to improve your awareness of it, and realign your mind and physical body
- Go from your toes to your feet, legs, pelvis, tummy, and so on until you reach the top of your head
- When you're completely relaxed, focus on the breath in and out and imagine it as white light moving through every cell of your body
- Embrace the light as it heals and strengthens you— positively glow with it
- When you're done, gently stretch back into your body, and reclaim physical control of it
- Do this ritual every time you want to realign your mind with your physical body and be sure to integrate with your favorite mantras or affirmations when you are done

ENERGY EXPELLING DANCING RITUAL— CHAOTIC MEDITATION

What you'll need:

* Your favorite music, preferably something rhythmic. You can also use traditional spiritual music, such as African Tribal Music, or Native Circle Dancing songs
* Plenty of room to move around

What you need to do:

* First, check in with your body. Notice any signs of tension you might be carrying. These are areas where negative energies can accumulate
* If you don't notice any physical tension, bring up any other emotions you're trying to expel, such as fear, or anger, or think of a specific event that impacted you negatively—bring out whatever you wish to expel
* When you're ready, start playing your music, and allow your body to move freely to it
* Don't think of any specific moves. Let your body lead the way. The mind is just the witness
* Move your body to the music, and imagine that every move helps expel negativity from your essence; shake it out!
* Do this for as long as it feels comfortable. At the end, you should feel refreshed, as if a weight has lifted off your shoulders

- Meditate while standing for a few minutes. Feel the lightness and freedom in your being and give gratitude
- Integrate with your mantras and affirmations

V

Your Tools

"A good tool improves the way you work. A great tool improves the way you think."

JEFF DUNTEMANN

WRITE YOUR OWN MAGIC—LET YOUR CREATIVITY FLOW!

Spells don't just appear in the world—they are created and conjured by a person with focused intention. An heirloom witch may often use "traditional" or "old" spells that have been written and passed down through generations, but these spells aren't necessarily more powerful than newer ones you find on the internet. What the older stuff does have is a history of energy that is precious. We can replicate that in a different way by calling to us our heroes, your ancestors who want the best for you, and all the people who would wish for the same outcome you are seeking. In the same way we call the corners, elements or Gods and Goddesses- we are presencing the spirit of that soul. They do answer. So do it with the open grace that only those who can come to be with you for both their and your highest good shall come.

Nothing is more powerful than what you can create for yourself when you are firmly grounded in your innate power. With magic, it's all about your own powers and energy. This will determine whether a spell is ultimately successful or not.

Powerful sorcerers and those who dedicate plenty of their time to their practice are able to achieve what they want by saying the right words. Others might want additional support:

- The right time and place
- Crystals
- Herbs
- Cords
- Energy-focusing methods like meditation or grounding

You don't have to make up your own spells if you don't want to. After all, you're always just a short search away from millions of spells. You even have lots to play with in this book.

But spell crafting could be beneficial for focusing your intentions. For one thing, when you create a spell yourself, you go through a transformation, as you study the problem you want to change in depth and try to determine the best magical avenue to approach it.

And this can allow you to understand what you actually want to accomplish. By the end, answers might be revealed to you, so it's critical for all magic practitioners to try, at least once, to craft their own spell.

Not only that, but a personalized spell has the added bonus of being more powerful to change the specific issue you want to address. Instead of taking the words or the steps of an existing spell, you are creating one just for the problem you want to change. You're building the solution, from scratch with your own special flavor.

THE BASIC STEPS OF A SPELL

Spells don't necessarily have to follow a very strict pattern or formula. Even a short prayer can be considered a spell, as long as the person saying it puts out a strong intention and uses their Magical Self to create change. Remember, a spell is just an arrangement of words. It's your intent and focus that makes it magical.

But if you're just getting started, following a more structured approach can help you understand what goes into creating and even casting a spell. Below, you can find some of the steps, but just remember that they don't necessarily have to apply to all magical spells, potions, or rituals:

1. THE NEED

Every spell wants to achieve something—or, more specifically, you want to achieve something through the spell.

Being as specific as possible makes for a stronger spell since it removes confusion and doubt. For instance, you can create a spell for "world peace," but that's pretty vague. How is world peace supposed to happen? What needs to be changed for the world to become peaceful?

The more specifically you can define the "need," the better. Then work to organize it in the positive. Rather than seeing the problem, see the result you wish to achieve.

2. THE TIME

Some spells need to be performed at a specific time. For instance, if you want to leverage the powers of the moon, then the spell should be performed at night. The phase of the moon could also be important, depending on what you want to achieve.

Maybe your spell is best performed during a particular season, when the herbs you need are in season. Fresh herbs are often more potent than dried or oils, but you can certainly make do with the latter too. Or perhaps you want the spell for an as-needed basis. In this case, you'll create the spell in such a way that time is not important for it.

I'm not going to provide much past the basics here because there are so many apps and resources that have already gone in depth on moon phases and astrology. Research what feels important to you. The more you put into it, the more you can expect from it. Provided your working is in the higher range of the frequency scale, of course.

3. THE WAY

The "way" here refers to the method and materials you will need to cast the spell.

There are several spellcasting methods to try. Some practitioners feel intuitively drawn to one; others try to use a diverse magical methodology and learn as much as possible.

This is a personal decision, though in the beginning, you should try to experiment a bit, to learn about which method works best for you.

Some magical methods include:

- Magical words - these are the prayers, poems, or "magical phrases" a spellcaster says to express their intent and make the change happen. Through words, you bring something from the inside (your mind) out into the world.

- Affirmations - they are similar to magical words, except they depend on repetition and emotion. You need to repeat an affirmation enough times for it to become reality, and the more you feel it, the easier the energy flows.

- Candle magic - relies on the light and power of the candle to allow your intent to come into being. The candle you choose must represent your purpose, as each color has its own meaning. If in doubt, use white.

- Cord magic - the cord is used to bind two elements, or transfer energy from one element to the other, depending on your intent.

- Potions - they rely on the powers of herbs and spices to create a frequency or attunement that supports and initiates inner change. Meaning the person who is drinking the potion is the one who will be ultimately affected by it.

- Spell jar – this is a potion or mixture that is not for consumption but to organize ingredients together to attune and harmonize for a goal. Oftentimes they are sealed with wax and buried or placed on an altar to work their magic.

- Journal magic – this is ridiculously potent when used properly. Fill your daily writings with gratitude for the things you wish to bring into reality. List the ways you already embody the wish or goal and continue to write about it day after day with a heart of gratitude and watch your manifestations come to life. These magical methods can be mixed and matched to your liking, of course, so don't feel like you must choose one over the other.

Once you decide the method for your spell, you can add "tools." These can be:

- Colors
- Shapes
- Types of herbs
- Powers of the elements (air, Earth, fire, water)
- Gods and Goddesses
- Crystals
- Materials (silk, cotton, paper)

Each of these can have their own meaning, which can help support your spell's purpose or take away from it.

Note that for a spell to work, it doesn't necessarily need a lot of tools or a combination of magical methods. Often, the most powerful spells are the simplest because they allow you to concentrate on the intent, and not the steps of the spell. Sometimes a simple tool for a focus that you take your time with can be the most potent.

3. THE ACTION

The next stage of a spell involves a symbolic action that represents the change you want to create. This is the catalyst that puts everything into motion.

In many cases, the symbolic action can involve the simple act of gathering all your ingredients, putting them together, and saying the words you want. Other spells can involve more complex actions, such as knot-tying, creating a circle, or setting an item on fire to symbolize purification.

Other examples of symbolistic actions can include:

- Writing and journaling
- Creating a spell jar
- Dancing
- Building a puppet
- Making a potion, tea, or cooking, etc.

The action itself is not important in the sense that, by its own, it does not define the spell. The intent and feeling that you put behind the action is what ultimately gives it power.

4. THE PURIFICATION

Once you have all the elements of the spell laid out, before you cast it, you must purify yourself, the space, or the elements you will use.

Purification is a crucial stage of any spell because it repels any negative energies that could interfere with your intent. For instance, many spells require you to meditate before you cast them, or even drink a purifying potion or take a shower to clear your mind and body. Showering with salt is a simple but powerful way to purify the body, especially cleaning the bends and crevices of the body with salt.

Objects that are supposed to hold onto energies (crystals, cords) must be purified because you reuse them. So does the room where you cast your spells since much of the negative energies you experience can become trapped in the physical space you're in. Be cautious using salt to cleanse a crystal because it can be so effective that it clears away any stored messages it might carry for you from the Earth. Sometimes just water and your focused white light is all you need.

Purification doesn't have to be complicated. You can meditate, cleanse the area by burning sage or palo santo, or even use a broom to symbolically sweep away energy that does not serve your intent. All of these are effective.

BRINGING IT ALL TOGETHER

Once you have all these four individual components, all you need to do is put them together and cast the spell. Once you are done, give great gratitude and release those that you called to you to lend you their energy and support. Close that circle and sit in gratitude for the successes that will soon appear.

On paper, spell crafting is pretty simple, though it will take a bit of time to learn what works and what doesn't. For now, you can use the spell formula below to help get you started.

This formula is essentially just a spell matrix that can be tailored to your specific intentions when needed. As you become more comfortable with your magical powers, you can confidently move beyond the matrix.

Eventually, we will move beyond all the rituals. But for now, embrace what you need to get you where you want to go.

SPELL MATRIX

- **WHAT I NEED TO CHANGE WITH MY SPELL:** ….

- **HOW I WILL CAST THE SPELL:**

  The magical method I'll use is: ....

  The tools I will need for my spells: ....

- **WHERE AND WHEN I WILL PERFORM MY SPELL:**
  …

- **PURIFICATION:** Cleanse the body before you cast a spell

My heart is free,
My conscience clear,
My body light,
With no bounds to fear.
My energy roams, unbound, so bright,
I am Divine, an action of light.
I allow my light to overflow,
In endless streams, my essence glows.
Thank you. Thank you. Thank you.

- **STATE YOUR INTENTION:**

    I cast this spell for [WHO] to [WHY/PURPOSE].

    I want to change [WHAT] because [REASON].

    This is my will. My will is to [WHO + WHY/ PURPOSE].

Example:

    *I cast this spell for [**friend's name**] to [**heal her broken heart**].*
    *I want to change [**emotional state**] because [**her pain is too much to bear**].*
    *This is my will. My will is to [**heal friend's name's broken heart**].*

State the intent out loud, to allow it to resonate through your energy.

- **ACTION:** Perform the spell using the methods and tools you've decided on.

If you aren't comfortable doing this yet, use script writing, one of the easiest spells around. Write down a few lines describing what happens after the spell comes true.

Example:

> **[Friend's name]** *came to me today. She was smiling and radiating pure happiness. She wanted to go traveling. She had so much energy. I have never seen her more joyful.*

- **END THE SPELL:** Restating your intent

[WHO+WHY/REASON]*

As I will it, so shall it be.

This time, state it as if it happened already.

Example:

[Friend's name] *heart is healed.*

As I will it, so shall it be.

GOODIES FOR YOUR TOOLBOX

"Nature has provided us a spectacular toolbox. The toolbox exists. An architect far better and smarter than us has given us that toolbox, and we now have the ability to use it."

BARRY SCHULER

These days, you can find a lot of ways to create your magical tool set. There are many people selling monthly boxes delivered to your doorstep, with dried herbs, crystals, and sigils made for you. If you would rather have someone else put together a spell jar or something for you, go for it. I bless and support their path to make money at something they are good at and yours to make your life easier. Whatever works for you.

These kits are not bad, and you can certainly purchase anything you want to help support your craft. But you can also cast pretty effective spells with the items you already have in your kitchen.

In this chapter, you will discover just a few of the very powerful tools to add to your craft, without needing to break the bank: herbs, spices, and the elements. There are some great books out there on magical herbology and crystals, and I encourage you to expand your library to include the classics if you haven't already. I'm going to include just a little bit of the basics here.

TOP MAGICAL HERBS TO USE IN SPELLS, POTIONS, RITUALS, AND MORE

BASIL

No pasta sauce is complete without basil, but this herb has a lot of great magical properties too. It is commonly used in love spells, but you'll find it in many potions designed for protection, such as for warding off small curses or hexes.

As a healer, it blocks calcium channels, which may help to lower blood pressure. It's great in tea because it has soothing effects and was used throughout history as a medicine for stomach pains.

CHAMOMILE

Most people use chamomile for its calming effects. It can help you unwind, soothe an upset stomach, and even put you in the perfect state to fall asleep.

From a magical perspective, chamomile is a powerful purification herb, used to cleanse the mind, body, and even energy. Chamomile brings balance. You can use it as a potion (tea), or carry it with you for protection.

CINNAMON

Cinnamon is considered an aphrodisiac, so it's a great spice for love spells and rituals. But it can also be used to cleanse a physical space, like your altar or the room where you cast your spells. Blow it through your door on the first of each month to bring in money.

If you carry it with you, cinnamon can help attract luck. Keep a small bag of it in your wallet, and you can attract wealth and abundance, when you need it.

Its healing properties include lowering blood sugar, and it has been known to assist those with diabetes when taken with a meal.

DANDELION

Dandelions are considered weeds by most people, but that's a shame. You can use the leaves, roots, and flowers as a potent liver tonic.

This flower has detoxifying properties and can be used to help cleanse the body and mind of negative energies. They are also used to help support the witch's intent and increase psychic powers before a spiritual interaction. Put it under your pillow, and the dandelion can help you banish nightmares.

LAVENDER

Lavender is a calming herb, which is why you'll see it in sleep-aiding teas, bags for anxiety, and body washes to help you relax.

Historically, it was also used to support passion and re-spark the flame of love in couples, and even as a negative energy repellant. It's got a list a mile long on its ability to soothe and calm and is used often for anything needing a little extra peace.

MINT

Mint has been used in magic for anything from attracting abundance and love, to enhancing one's well-being and adding clarity to one's path.

Most people may indulge in a cup of mint tea when they have an upset stomach. This is because mint can be very soothing and calming. It can also assist with headaches. If placed under a pillow, it can help you induce a psychic dream or protect you in your sleep against nightmares.

MUGWORT

Mugwort is used as a "treatment" for fatigue and to prepare for long journeys. Some witches and psychics also use it to help induce lucid dreaming and astral traveling because the herb has some psychoactive properties.

It's also a very versatile herb, and you can use it in tea blends as well as creams, or incense to help with digestive problems, irregular menstruation, and high blood pressure.

NUTMEG

Nutmeg can symbolize peace, clarity, and help with healing. It's a potent anti-inflammatory. It was commonly used as a wedding blessing, to help new happy couples build a happy life together and keep their love strong.

You'll find nutmeg in a lot of love spells, as well as those for luck, drawing money, banishing conflict, or even promoting a restful sleep.

POPPY

Poppy has been used for centuries to induce psychic visions, as well as erase grief and suffering. The latter actually comes from Greek mythology, when the Goddess Demeter was given poppy to heal her broken heart after her daughter Persephone was abducted.

In fact, many of the magical properties of herbs and spices have their roots in the world's mythology.

ROSEMARY

Rosemary is another staple in many of the world's kitchens. For a witch, burning rosemary before a spell is a way to increase their powers and strengthen their intent. You can also use it to eliminate negativity or purify a space.

But rosemary is most strongly associated with a strong will, so it's commonly used in spells where you need to remove doubts from someone's heart.

SAGE

Sage is one of the most well-known cleansing herbs around, but it's a bit misleading.

White sage is the herb you use for cleansing. It's often burned, and the smoke that emanates from it can release any negative presence trapped in a space.

Common sage, the kind you find in any grocery store, is used to promote wisdom and clear the mind. Just one cup of sage tea, combined with a bit of meditation, can help you remove doubts and see your path more clearly, so definitely try it!

THYME

Thyme is a symbol of bravery and strength, so it's used a lot in spells designed to increase someone's courage.

It also has preservation properties, as it was used by the ancient Egyptians during the mummification process. Symbolically, thyme can help prevent things from changing. It's been used to help bacterial and fungal infections and has been said to have potent antioxidant effects.

VERVAIN

Roman soldiers would carry some vervain when going into battle as they believed it had protective properties. Witches use it both for purification spells and protection. You'll commonly find some types of love spells where the lover needs to reveal a truth hidden within their subconscious.

Vervain has been attributed for the relief of many conditions including kidney stones, jaundice, gout, headaches, anxiety, depression, and insomnia.

MAGICAL HERBS AND SPICES GLOSSARY

- Agrimony - healing, restoration, and protection
- Alfalfa - attracting abundance, cleansing, promoting good fortune
- Astragalus - health, mental clarity and focus, shielding
- Bay leaf - wisdom, strength
- Bearberry - psychic visions and dreams
- Birch Bark - protection, strength, kickstart new beginnings
- Calendula - bringing to light old memories, honoring those who've passed
- Catnip - attracting love, feline magic, blessing one's familiar
- Cedar - wisdom, protection, power, strength
- Comfrey - luck (especially for travelers), healing
- Damiana - sex magic, energy work
- Devil's Claw - protection, keeping evil away
- Dill - protection against illness
- Elderberry - wisdom, banishing
- Eucalyptus - cleansing, healing
- Fennel Seeds - protection, confidence
- Ginger - passion and love, success
- Hibiscus - love, confidence, independence
- Irish Moss - attracting abundance
- Jasmine - attracting love and increasing one's sensuality, kindness

- Licorice Root - gaining an advantage, power, domination
- Mandrake - protection, love, removing curses
- Marshmallow Root - increase psychic powers, protection, connecting with good spirits
- Mistletoe - good love, love, money
- Nettle - courage, healing, banishing evil
- Orange Peel - blessing, good luck
- Patchouli - love and sex, fertility
- Pine - prosperity, good health, persistence
- Raspberry Leaves - love, tempting others
- Red Sandalwood - meditation, healing, entering a trance state
- Rose - love, harmony, offerings to Gods and Goddesses
- Rue - warding, attracting love, cleansing
- Valerian - enemy spells, removing negative energies
- White Willowbark - wisdom, love
- Wild Lettuce - inducing dreams and vision
- Witch Hazel - comfort, wisdom, removing anger and soothing the heart
- Wormwood - banishing evil spirits, reversing curses and spells
- Yarrow - courage, good fortune

HOW TO USE THESE HERBS AND SPICES

There are no wrong or right ways to use herbs and spices, or even other tools in your magical practice.

Yes, all of these tools may have their own symbolism, but at the end of the day, they're just that: tools. Magic ultimately obeys your will, and all of the other accessories you can purchase or cultivate are ways for you to focus on your intent and powers, so that your will is executed.

Ultimately, the intent behind your spell is what matters most. But to help get you started, here are a few different ways you can use herbs and spices in your craft:

POTIONS/TEAS

The simplest way to use these herbs and spices is to make a potion or a tea, and drink it.

You can use a combination of herbs, depending on what you want the potion to help with. Remember, the herbs themselves have magical properties on their own, but they require you to "activate" them.

Meditating before you drink the tea or combining it with other spells and rituals are a simple way to activate the herbs and feel their magical effects.

*Be sure to double-check the edibility of all herbs you wish to consume and make sure you do not ingest anything toxic.

FOOD/COOKING

Many people don't think of food as magical, but what else can you call it? It fills your tummy and your heart and allows you energy to get through the day. The foods you eat can make you happy, or soothe you when going through a bad time. They can heal you and give strength.

So don't be afraid to add these herbs and spices to your food to sprinkle some extra magic!

CREAMS AND OINTMENTS

Herbs and spices with healing properties can be made into a cream or ointment, and applied directly to the skin. The act can be medicinal, or even ritualistic if you want to tap more into the magical powers of the herbs.

It's perfectly alright to purchase creams and ointments from the store, but you can also make them yourself at home and create your own ritual. Mix the herbs and spices with some oil in a bowl and apply it to any area that needs soothing.

ESSENTIAL OILS

A lot of spells will ask for fresh or at least dry herbs. The fresher they are, the more potent their effects can be.

However, sometimes buying fresh herbs is not an option. Whether they're not in season or you can't find access to them, essential oils can be a convenient alternative to any modern witch.

Oil can be added to spell jars, ritualistic baths, and some of them can even be ingested, so you can add a few drops to your tea or coffee. A good, medicinal-quality oil can be far more potent than a dried herb that has lost its luster. If gathered and created right, the frequency of the herb's life is captured in the oil.

SPELL JARS

Most spells don't have an immediate effect. They need time to work their magic, or are designed to have a long-term effect, in which case you will need to keep a token from the spell around.

Spell jars are a fantastic way to add some magic to your home and use these herbs and spices at their full value. You can include other magical tools as well, such as crystals, rocks, charms, and personal objects like jewelry or photos.

CHARMS

Think of charms as tiny to-go spells. They're used mostly for protective purposes, but you can create a charm to fulfill any need, such as attracting good fortune or luck.

You don't need to unleash your DIY master to make a charm, unless you want to. Just add a few herbs and spices to a tiny bag, seal it, and carry it with you in your pocket or purse.

DECORATIONS

If you're worried about publicly displaying your magic, don't be. There are lots of ways to blend your magical side with your mundane world.

For instance, you can keep potted plants in your home. The live plants will continue to fill your home with their magical powers, hidden in plain sight.

Or dry some flowers and hang them on your walls, or stick them to a canvas. It's a lovely piece of decoration that fills your home with magic!

THE FOUR ELEMENTS

Apart from those herbs and spices, you also have four extremely potent tools by your side:

Earth

Air

Fire

Water

Each of these four elements make up the reality you live in, so they can be used to change it, give more power to your spells, and even help form a stronger intent.

You will likely feel drawn to one element in particular, as they each correspond to certain zodiac signs. In the next section, you can learn all about the elements, when to use them, and even different objects that represent them:

Earth

When to use this element:

- Fertility
- Attracting abundance
- Supporting / changing physical reality
- Blessing the harvest

Best time to perform spells:

- Winter
- Midnight

Crystals and rocks:

- Salt
- Agate
- Smoky quartz
- Emerald
- Bloodstone

Zodiac signs:

- Capricorn
- Virgo
- Taurus

Colors:

- Green
- White
- Black
- Brown

Incense:

- Storax
- Benzoin

Plants:

- Barley
- Ivy
- Corn
- Oak
- Oats
- Rye
- Wheat

Air

When to use this element:

- Psychic work
- Learn, acquire knowledge
- Become more creative, get ideas
- Unlock memories
- Heal the mind

Best time to perform spells:

- Spring
- Dawn

Crystals:

- Topaz
- Fluorite
- Citrine

Zodiac signs:

- Gemini
- Aquarius
- Libra

Colors:

- White
- Blue
- Yellow
- Pastels

Incense:

- Frankincense
- Myrrh
- Fumitory

Plants:

- Plants and trees
  that provide incense
- Aspen
- Windflower

Fire

When to use this element:

- Purification
- Sex magic
- Increase motivation
- Boost energy
- Spark love, passion (sex, in life)
- Remove anger
- Increase power and influence
- Purify and heal

Best time to perform spells:

- Noon
- Summer

Crystals:

- Amethyst
- Firestone
- Fire opal

Zodiac signs:

- Leo
- Aries
- Sagittarius

Colors:

- White
- Orange
- Red
- Crimson

Incense:

- Rose
- Frankincense
- Copal

Plants:

- Rose
- Red poppy
- Onions
- Peppers
- Mustard
- Garlic
- Almond trees

Water

When to use this element:

- Healing and purification
- Psychic work
- Love spells
- Increase sensuality
- Remove negative emotions (sorrow, pain, melancholy)
- Support fertility
- Promote change

Best time to perform spells:

- Fall
- Twilight

Crystals:

- Coral
- Sea salt
- Jade

Zodiac signs:

- Cancer
- Scorpio
- Pisces

Colors:

- Blue
- Black
- Green

Incense:

- Lotus
- Myrrh

Plants:

- Seaweed
- Water lily
- Willow
- Moss
- Lotus
- Fungi

PRACTICES TO ENHANCE YOUR JOURNEY

"Practice isn't the thing you do once you're good. It's the thing you do that makes you good."

MALCOLM GLADWELL

Spells, rituals, potions, affirmations—these are just some of the many tools in a sorcerer's arsenal.

In this last section, you can discover some powerful (and even fun) magical activities that can help you become even more in tune with your magical abilities.

HOOPONOPONO – MAGIC AT ITS BEST

"Holding onto anger is like drinking poison and expecting the other person to die."

ORIGINAL AUTHOR UNKNOWN

What do you normally think of forgiveness? Is it a sign of weakness, or one of the greatest symbols of love?

Well, to Hawaiians, forgiveness is a way of restoring balance both in a group, and even oneself. We spoke earlier about forgiveness being the main path out of harmful karmas.

Ho'oponopono, the ancient practice of forgiveness, roughly means "to make things become rebalanced." It's a very simple ritual that can help cleanse a person of all negative emotions, from shame to guilt, anger, resentment, and those deep hidden blocks that keep us from our highest path.

It's a release of negativity which you may harbor toward others, or even yourself. It will empower you to work your magic free from frequencies that disempower your efforts.

And to perform this ritual, you essentially have to utter four key phrases:

I'm sorry.
Please forgive me.
Thank you.
I love you.

That's it.

Of course, you can meditate on what or who you're forgiving, to give this ritual a little more direction and feel its effects better.

But with regular practice, you can begin to develop a better sense of self-love even without having a specific event or person to focus on.

MANIFESTATION MEDITATION

Meditating is a powerful tool that can help you become more aware of your thought patterns, calibrate your energy levels, and even focus your intent right before casting a spell.

Meditation is magical in its own right, and can be used to create change, just like casting a spell.

This change can be internal. As you meditate you bring awareness to your thought patterns and try to heal your mind. Reciting affirmations or mantras while you meditate can shift your consciousness. They can also change your perception, and lead to more positive outlooks on life.

But, through manifestation meditation, you can create change from within the "self."

Here's how to do a very basic manifesting meditation:

- Find a comfortable and quiet space where you can focus
- Lie down in any position you want
- Breathe in and out through your nose. As best as you can, try to focus only on your breath
- If any thoughts try to distract you, let them pass by
- After a few minutes, bring up a specific goal you want to manifest
- Put the goals into a few words, such as "I am at peace" or "I attract money effortlessly"
- Then, begin to visualize your goal, as if you've reached it already
- Make it as vivid as possible
- Repeat your goal a few times, out loud or in your mind

You can perform a manifesting meditation any time you want. The more you do it, the faster you'll see its effects.

CONSCIOUS BREATHING

Conscious breathing is a technique that helps you become more aware of your breath. It's a great way to ground yourself right before performing a spell or ritual, or any time you want to quiet the mind.

Over time, practicing conscious breathing helps you become more calm and present, so that you can engage more deeply with all aspects of your life.

There are a lot of conscious breathing techniques, but by far the simplest one involves just three steps:

- Sit in a comfortable position
- Put a hand on your chest and one on your stomach
- Inhale and exhale deeply, while feeling the air come in and out, and your hands moving

That's it!

Well, not really but it's a great start.

You can also count your inhale and exhales, which can help you stay focused, or look at a specific object in your room to create a better sense of awareness of your physical placement.

I could write an entire book on breathing. It's the thing we do the most in our life, and it's the thing we focus on the least. There is so much power in the breath, but because it's so normal, we miss the sacredness of it. If you spent your entire life on just the study of the breath, it would be a life well spent.

JOURNALING

Can you perceive that there may be more amazing things in your life than you are aware of? Negative events tend to take up a lot more space, which can easily lead to the belief that your life is void of anything beautiful or valuable.

Well, journaling can be a great way to change this perspective. The act of writing forces you to think of your life differently. For one thing, by default, you are putting events into order, and are able to trace them like a story. If you only write down the bad stuff, you will magnify it and create more of that.

But when you write things down, it's much easier to see that some specific event that causes you worry or anxiety isn't as serious as you initially thought. In fact, it's just a small entry in a page.

But from a magical perspective, journaling can bring balance and clarity to your journey. The technique itself can become its own type of spell, which you can use to put things into cosmic motion.

Journaling can seem difficult if you make a big deal out of it. Try to distance yourself from any preconceived notions of what a journal is, or the type of style you need to write in.

Here are some tips that can help get you started:

- Commit to writing for just five minutes a day in the

beginning and if you feel like writing more keep going. You don't have to make a whole plan of it for the perfect place and the perfect way. Just write.

- Write about what makes you grateful, happy, and passionate. Write about things that make you feel good. The things you can be proud of yourself for. The things you cherish in those around you.

- Ideally, writing the old-fashioned way (with a pen) helps interact your brain with your subconscious mind best but choose a format you're most comfortable with. If it's a laptop, one of the many apps out there, or even your phone's notes app just make a place that is just for your journaling.

- Meditate for a few minutes before you start writing, and start with a specific topic or question, such as, "What did I do right today?" "What am I grateful for?"

- Start writing without censoring yourself. Ignore grammar mistakes, typos, or whether the sentences make sense together.

There is no limit to what you can write about. Journaling is a way to allow some inner thoughts to get out, so allow them to exist without polishing them!

YOGA

The word means "to yoke." To become one with the One. Today, many people turn to yoga as a way to move their body and reap the physical benefits. It is lovely to be able to tie your own shoes when you are in your 80s, but don't forget—yoga is a spiritual practice that can help reveal your magical side as well! When you study yoga in depth, it teaches supernormal powers and techniques in the Yoga Sutras.

Yoga is an ancient science that aims to strengthen the connection between the body, mind, and spirit. Its goal is to help you look inward and become more connected with yourself, and the Supreme Consciousness—or the Magical Self!

The movements in yoga are controlled and purposeful. They are each designed to activate certain energy points through the body, and often invite practitioners to deeper reflections.

Some yoga poses to try can include:

LOTUS POSE - to calm the mind and prepare you for deep meditation

Sit on the floor, with your back straight. Bring your left ankle to the crease of your right hip, with your foot's sole facing the sky. Repeat with your right leg, so that both legs go one over the other, like so:

WARRIOR POSE - to overcome ego and ignorance, and strengthen courage

Bring your right foot forward, with your legs pointing straight. Take your left foot and extend it backward, as much as it feels comfortable. Then, stretch your arms over your head, and connect your palms like so:

CHILD'S POSE - allows your energy to rest and discard negative energy. The pose mimics the childlike appeal of surrendering

Kneel to the ground with your legs tucked underneath. Rest your torso on your thighs, and stretch your arms forward:

TREE POSE - to achieve balance, increase awareness of the body

Keep one foot firmly on the ground and connect the sole of the other foot to your calf. You can connect your hands to your front, or back like so:

Your body will move slightly in this pose, and that's okay. Much like a tree, your "root" is firmly planted in the ground, while all your branches and leaves on top are free to move.

There are countless other poses you can try, so feel free to explore the magical world of yoga! Just remember that the goal is not to achieve the "perfect" pose, so don't be hard on yourself if you can't keep the position for long or need to modify it a bit.

The goal is alignment between your mind, body, and spirit. This takes time, so take it slow. Give yourself the space to improve your pose, with no judgment!

DANCING

Dancing is linked to many ancient traditions as more than just a way to have fun or exercise. It's a ritual in its own right, used to express devotion, heal, remove negative energies, and reconnect with one's magical self.

This act symbolizes a transference of energy. The ear connects with the energy of the sound, which fills the entire body and makes it move. The sound itself creates an effect on the body, mind, and spirit.

It's why you feel happy and in a good mood when you listen to positive music. When you're sad, listening to a soul-crushing ballad can help you release some of that emotion you bottle up within you.

In magic, dancing does not follow a rule. You don't need specific steps or choreography—you just need to allow your body to move as it wants, to a specific sound. It doesn't even have to be music. The sound of the woods, if you truly listen to them, can make your body start to move gently as if it were a branch swinging in the wind.

You can use dancing for anything you want. Like all magical tools, it follows your intent, to the letter.

WISHING YOU WELL TILL WE MEET AGAIN

I hope that you never stop learning about your magical self, or stop discovering new avenues of its power. Sure, your learning might slow down from time to time, but I hope that it never stops. You are an incredible, Divine being of light and power, and your will for a better life for yourself and those around you is a blessing to all of us.

You should take immense joy every single time you learn something new, create a spell, or take part in a new ritual. These are proof that the world is full of gifts, all of which await for you to reach out and grab them. Enjoy the journey without the burden of reaching the end. This is the secret to a life well lived.

I look forward to continuing with you on your amazing journey, and I hope to see you online or in the ethers as we work together to heal ourselves and our planet. It's been a privilege to work with you here with you, and when you are in your practice, know that you are never alone.

You CAN control your own destiny.

You have the POWER to achieve anything you want.

And together, we WILL change the world for the better.

Please continue the journey by joining us at www.evolutionarymagic.com or scan the barcode below for your members-only access that will take you to a place with the spells and rituals from this book as well as a bunch of new treasures.

The journey continues...

Join the Magic

Acknowledgments

With deep appreciation, I bow to all of those who have the courage to follow their path even when it is dramatically upstream from society. May you always feel known and treasured.

I am eternally grateful for my God-Father, Spirit, ancestors, guides, and the angels along the way who make this life worth living. I am thankful to the never-ending internal nudge to share and grow with this amazing world and I am thankful to the people in my life who encourage me to do just that. They are the heart of my heart and they know who they are. And always and forever... thank you, David, the one who lights up my world.

A special thank you is in order for Catalina M. because without her this work would not be possible. May you always walk in joy and light.

ABOUT THE AUTHOR

Beneath the surface of a life marked by traditional constraints, C. L. Biggs, MS, RMT, always felt the pull of something deeper—a call from the Spirit that defied the rigid boundaries of her upbringing. From a young age, she wrestled with the tension between her innate magical gifts and the teachings she was surrounded by. This journey of reconciling religion with spirituality and science with magic has shaped her into a beacon for those seeking to break free from limiting beliefs and embrace a harmonious blend of intellect and intuition.

Guided by a profound desire to uplift the world, C. L. Biggs embarked on a transformative path of learning and discovery. Her journey led her through rigorous training in Kinesiology, Hypnotherapy, Reiki, and Religious Studies, where she cultivated a deep understanding of the human mind and spirit. Furthering her knowledge, she earned advanced Criminal Justice and Psychology degrees from the University of Central Florida. However, it was a career-ending diagnosis that became the catalyst for her greatest transformation. Embracing the Mystic Arts and Quantum Sciences, she expanded her teachings, guiding diverse audiences from Florida to Washington State with wisdom, humor, and a light-hearted approach.

In her debut work from the *Magical Series*, C. L. Biggs masterfully intertwines ancient wisdom with modern science, offering readers a portal to their own divine potential. Through her writing, she invites us all to explore the magic within, reminding us that the journey of self-discovery is best undertaken with curiosity, joy, and an open heart.

For more information, go to:

www.clbiggs.com

Frequency Chart of Consciousness

Dr. David Hawkins

	Name of Level	Energetic Log	Predominant Emotional State	View of Life	God-view	Process
Spiritual Paradigm	Enlightenment	700-1000	Ineffable	Is	Self	Pure Consciousness
	Peace	600	Bliss	Perfect	All-Being	Illumination
	Joy	540	Serenity	Complete	One	Transfiguration
	Love	500	Reverence	Benign	Loving	Revelation
Reason & Integrity	Reason	400	Understanding	Meaningful	Wise	Abstraction
	Acceptance	350	Forgiveness	Harmonious	Merciful	Transcendence
	Willingness	310	Optimism	Hopeful	Inspiring	Intention
	Neutrality	250	Trust	Satisfactory	Enabling	Release
	Courage	200	Affirmation	Feasible	Permitting	Empowerment
Survival Paradigm	Pride	175	Scorn	Demanding	Indifferent	Inflation
	Anger	150	Hate	Antagonistic	Vengeful	Aggression
	Desire	125	Craving	Disappointing	Denying	Enslavement
	Fear	100	Anxiety	Frightening	Punitive	Withdrawal
	Grief	75	Regret	Tragic	Disdainful	Despondency
	Apathy	50	Despair	Hopeless	Condemning	Abdication
	Guilt	30	Blame	Evil	Vindictive	Destruction
	Shame	20	Humiliation	Miserable	Despising	Elimination

OMEGA

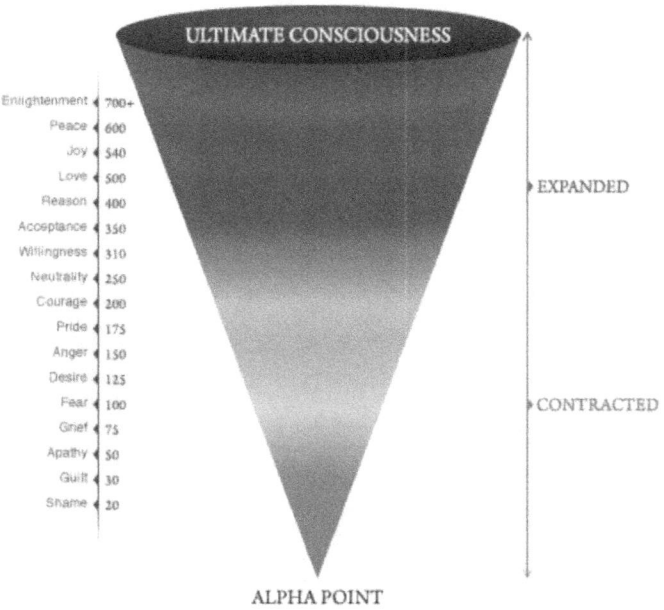

ULTIMATE CONSCIOUSNESS

Enlightenment ◄ 700+
Peace ◄ 600
Joy ◄ 540
Love ◄ 500
Reason ◄ 400
Acceptance ◄ 350
Willingness ◄ 310
Neutrality ◄ 250
Courage ◄ 200
Pride ◄ 175
Anger ◄ 150
Desire ◄ 125
Fear ◄ 100
Grief ◄ 75
Apathy ◄ 50
Guilt ◄ 30
Shame ◄ 20

EXPANDED

CONTRACTED

ALPHA POINT